Record labels from VP / Randy's Records

Miss Pat

My Reggae Music Journey

FROM MENTO, SKA, ROCKSTEADY, REGGAE TO DANCEHALL

DOROTHY PATRICIA CHIN O.D.

Miss Pat
My Reggae Music Journey

FROM MENTO, SKA, ROCKSTEADY, REGGAE TO DANCEHALL

66 "What Berry Gordy
was to Motown Records,

what Russell Simmons
was to Def Jam Recordings,

what Sylvia Robinson
was to Sugar Hill Records,

what Clive Davis
was to Arista Records,

Patricia Chin
is to the Reggae industry,
and VP Records."

Kool Herc
"The Founder of Hip-Hop"

Miss Pat in front of the Unisphere in Flushing Meadows, Queens (Corona Park)

Downtown Kingston, Jamaica

Dedication

To my extended family for being part of who I am.

To my late mother and father for preparing me for all that life brought.

To Gregory and Joel—you will forever live on in my heart.

To my children, grandchildren, and great-grandchildren—may you always have music in your lives.

Finally, to my late husband, Vincent "Randy" Chin, for sharing with me an adventure like no other.

Miss Pat, My Reggae Music Journey:
From Mento, Ska, Rocksteady, Reggae to Dancehall

Photography Copyright: Blue Sun Films, Simon Buckland,
Beth Lesser, Ted Bafaloukos, Anderson Ballantyne,
Alessandro Simonetti, David Corio, Peter Simon, Ebet Roberts,
Marlon 'Ajamu' Myrie, Kim Gottlieb-Walker, Roy Sweetland,
David Muir, Monika Campbell, William Richards, Gussie Clarke,
Allan Tannenbaum, Carter Van Pelt, Maria Papaefstathiou,
Michael Thompson, Paul Hawthorne, Johnny Nunez, and
Jose Guerra.
Writers: Anicée Gaddis, John Masouri, Alex Lee, and
James "Jazz" Goring
Developmental Editors: Janice Julian, Aaron Talbert and Chris Chin
Copyeditors: Dawn Hugh and Camille Lee-Chin
Editorial Assistance: Stephanie Chin and Barry Wilson
Legal Clearances: John McQueeney, Esq.
Proofreaders: Linsey Doering and Shivaun Hearne
Foreword: Dr. Carolyn Cooper, C.D.
Artwork: Michael Thompson and Maria Papaefstathiou
Cover Artwork: Michael Thompson
Cover and Interior Design: Maria Papaefstathiou
Photo Editor: Nikos Glykeas
Coordination and Production: Maria Papaefstathiou, James "Jazz"
Goring, Aaron Talbert, Lorenzo Sukhu, Chris O'Brien and Barry Wilson.

Printed in Greece, Pressious Arvanitidis Printing Co.

First Printing, 2020
ISBN: 978-0-578-65725-7
Library of Congress: 2020905087

Published & Distributed by: VP Music Group, 89-05 138th Street,
Jamaica, New York 11435

Distributed by: Gingko Press, 2332 4th St., Ste E, Berkeley, CA 94710

Contents

Fore word

"Life On a Big Screen"

Miss Pat's Stellar Journey

by Carolyn Cooper

In "Gone A Foreign", the third chapter of her illuminating autobiography, Mrs. Patricia Chin, affectionately known as Miss Pat, describes her first view of New York City in this vivid way: "It was just on an exaggerated scale for us, like life on a big screen."

It's no overstatement to say that Miss Pat's own story would make an inspiring documentary. Coming from a small island to the big city, Miss Pat brought all the elements of a great script. It's a classic success story. Born in humble circumstances, she learnt valuable lessons from her parents who motivated her to achieve. They taught her how to value family which has been the foundation of her remarkable life.

Miss Pat also learned at home how to be enterprising: to turn her hand mek fashion, as we say in Jamaica. Taking the little she had and making a profit by investing it wisely! It all started with selling marbles to her classmates to earn lunch money.

Much later, Miss Pat and her husband Vincent 'Randy' Chin recognised the economic power of Jamaican popular music. They went into the business of culture. Randy's Record Mart was established in 1958 at 17 North Parade, downtown Kingston. Then a production studio was added.

In the 1970s, the Chins migrated to the U.S. and in 1979 the VP Records label was born. From the town of Kings to the borough of Queens, VP Records has remained the Independent Label of choice for reggae music. As Orville 'Shaggy' Burrell says, "The good thing about VP was that they was our outlet. Because now all the majors are buying into our music. But back then, VP was our only outlet. They was that little candle light at the end of the tunnel."

In 2015, when VP Records celebrated its 35th anniversary at the Grace Jerk Festival in Queens, Miss Pat was in her element. She was a ball of energy bouncing around the venue. The showpiece of the event was a vibrant pop-up exhibition on Jamaican popular music, brilliantly designed by graphic artist Michael 'Freestylee' Thompson, co-founder with Maria Papaefstathiou of the International Reggae Poster Contest. Huge banners, featuring iconic Jamaican musicians, attracted thousands of visitors to the VP tent.

Miss Pat has been a visionary supporter of the International Reggae Poster Contest, attending exhibitions in the U.S., Mexico, Spain, Cuba and Jamaica. I met her in 2013 at the opening of a poster exhibition at the Multitudes Gallery in Little Haiti, Miami. I saw her again at another exhibition of posters at the Organization of American States in Washington, D.C.

"Miles ahead in reggae music." That's the VP trademark. And it's been quite a journey for Miss Pat. VP is now the biggest distributor of reggae, dancehall and soca music. To di world! Miss Pat's inspiring autobiography documents her vital contribution to the growth of VP Records and the music industry in Jamaica. Nuff respect due, Miss Pat!

Montego Bay

Jamaica
LAND OF MY BIRTH

Kingston

It is the summer of 2015 and the American Association of Independent Music (A2IM) is honoring me with their coveted Lifetime Achievement Award.

I have always felt proud to be a woman. So as I take my 4'11" "tallawah" self on stage and wave at the cheering crowd now on their feet, I accept the award for all women—short and tall—working their way up a male-dominated field. It is a journey I know all too well. But I want more company on that stage. This is why I encourage female artists to keep trying. This is why I tell young women that they can do more than take care of their home and children. I tell them they can run a home and business at the same time if they really want to. "Just start where you are," I always say. "The rest will follow."

May 8, 2004, was another day I'll never forget. I was in a limo with my children heading to Radio City Music Hall to celebrate VP Records' twenty-fifth anniversary. As we approached the iconic theater, I saw my name in bright lights on the marquee above the people standing in line waiting to get into the concert. It was the first time I had ever been in a limo and the first time I would walk a red carpet. I couldn't stop marveling at the fact that all these people had come out to celebrate this special occasion with me. Was this really happening? As I took a deep breath, my mind flashed back to when I was just ten—almost seventy years earlier—when my father used to put my mother on his bicycle handlebars to take her to the movies on the weekends. As children, we'd run after them crying because we wanted to go, too. I guess we didn't understand that you can't fit five on a bicycle. The Radio City night reminded me just how far I had come. That's what music does. It gives you the power of time travel.

Miss Pat at A2IM Lifetime Achievement Award (2015)

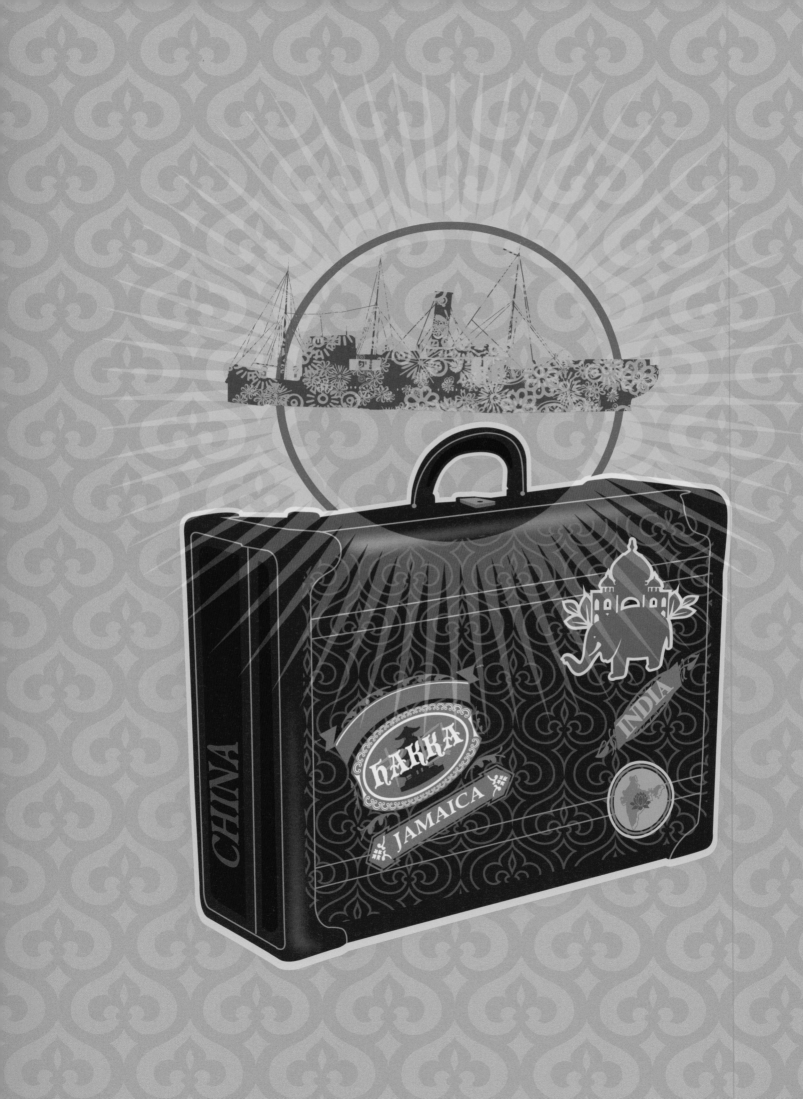

Part One

Early Life

1937-1957

"As a woman, she's a born survivor; she make things happen as a lady inna this business. She's a workaholic, and everybody like her; she help a man keep the wheels rolling, and all now Miss Pat's business a roll. Miss Pat help the whole of we; you would have said the Godfather, but she ah the Godlady fi all of we, she helpful and she responsible for all of us, like Bunny Lee, Lee Perry, Linford Anderson and Clancy Eccles. Miss Pat give all of we a push start and she treat us pon the same level. She is one of the greatest, and any man say otherwise, I can testify it's a lie them a tell. Anybody in the record business that sell records, come right up, they don't have a bad thing to say about Miss Pat."

Bunny "Striker" Lee

Dorothy Patricia Williams

I was born Dorothy Patricia Williams in Kingston, Jamaica, on September 20, 1937. My mother was full Chinese and my father full East Indian. Both sets of grandparents were immigrants who started their new lives in the West Indies with nothing.

Perhaps spurred on by this common background, sparks flew when my parents met. They married after a short courtship much to the dismay of my maternal grandparents. In those days, marrying outside of one's culture was considered an act of defiance. Now an outcast, my mother left her family's home and made a life with her husband. She brought three children into this world and passed on her rebel gene to at least one of the three. As the firstborn—the daughter my father named after a movie star he admired—I was expected to help take care of my younger brother, Harry, and sister, Cynthia, and set an example for them. Growing up, I always had that in the back of my mind.

Our close-knit family started out in life poor in material things but rich in optimism. The one-room home we lived in had—although just barely—everything we needed for survival. For starters, it had the bed on which the five of us slept. Sitting next to the bed atop a small round table was our only source of light—an old kerosene lamp bearing the words Home Sweet Home. Next to this was a small chest of drawers with a mirror attached. At the end of the room was a tiny dining table. And at the foot of the bed was a narrow armoire of sorts that stored the few articles of clothing we owned. Because it had no door, we used a piece of cloth to protect our clean clothes from dust. The bathroom and kitchen, of course, were outside. But as crammed as it was in there, we still had to make room for our bicycle. At night, right before turning out the lamp, Mom and we kids would get into the bed so that my father could bring the bicycle in, squeeze it into the narrow space between the bed and the armoire, and shut the door.

Important Influences

Entertainment, at least by today's standards, was practically nonexistent. Luckily for us, we had one or two neighbors wealthy enough to afford a radio. When we weren't busy with chores, we would stand outside their home and listen to the broadcasts through the open doors or windows. Despite our lack of material comforts or distractions, however, there was never time for boredom or complaints. Whenever she could, my mother would share stories about her hardworking shopkeeper parents and the innovative tricks they used to do business with their customers despite the language barrier. Always industrious, she made us learn practical skills such as cooking and sewing, while on our own my siblings and I would make toys, like slingshots. On Saturdays, we'd go to see our father at the haberdashery store where he worked six days a week. I remember rubber bands and marbles being the new novelty item back then. Because my dad could get them in bulk,

Miss Pat's mother, Mama Chi-Chi

Miss Pat's father, Joe

Miss Pat's family.
Top L to R: Father, Mother, Tee (cousin)
Middle L to R: Pat, Cynthia (sister),
Harry (brother).
Front: Winston (cousin).

Friends and family. Top L to R: Friends.
Middle L to R: Cynthia (sister), Mom, Aunt Edna, Harry (brother). Front: Pat

Miss Pat (age 17)

he'd give me a few, which I'd then sell at school for my lunch money. It was while selling those rubber bands and marbles that I made the connection between turning a profit and having fun. That's when I got my first taste for entrepreneurship. I felt the joy in providing something that others loved and making pocket change for my effort. Before long, a second influence would begin to make its mark on me: music.

We were living on Fifth Street in an area called Greenwich Farm. On Sun-

days, with no real brick-and-mortar building to call church, the community would hold a roadside makeshift service on the main road where they'd sing and shake their tambourines. My parents would allow our neighbors to take my sister and me to the service, the clap-hand church, which is how the weekly ritual and musical influence became a part of our foundation years. I would learn years later that we weren't the only ones in the community influenced by the music and singing. I didn't know them then, but within

walking distance from our house lived several young musicians, and one boy in particular by the name of Bunny Lee. A few years my junior, he would also feel the pull of music and eventually go on to become a major force as a record producer, as well as my friend.

One day, when my sister, Cynthia, and I were seven and nine respectively, our mother decided that we needed piano lessons. I will never know the reason why, but it was as if she felt instinctively that music was going to be important for us. Grateful that Mom had made this possible, we jumped at the opportunity to learn something new and took lessons after school from her piano-teacher friend. Soon after, with ready-to-wear clothes not yet widely available, Mom added dressmaking to our list of skills, no doubt in anticipation of her daughters working in a shop while raising a family. By age twelve I was producing a dress a week on my very own sewing machine, with each creation featuring more intricate detailing than the one before. The last thing I wanted was a normal dress. I didn't want normal anything, a conviction that clearly played out in my life. Even at that young age, the desire to be different was strong in me. It may have seemed like a simple task, but learning how to sew gave me an outlet for my creative side, while the discipline it required strengthened the tendency I already had to finish what I started. Even as a little girl, once I started something I became obsessed with it. I have no doubt that this attitude helped me in my life and career.

The Women Ahead of Me

My mother was not the only strong female influence in my life. Aunt Edith, my father's sister, lived just across the way from us. She was a tough cookie, a result, I believe, of the hard childhood she and my father endured. When she was just an infant and my father was four, their mother passed away. Their father, a deeply spiritual man, did his best to take care of them. He would soon remarry and give his children a stepmother. But as their new mother battled severe alcoholism, life remained difficult. Then, when Aunt Edith and my father were just eight and twelve respectively, tragedy struck again. One night while they were sleeping, robbers broke into their shop and home and shot and killed my grandfather as he tried to protect his family. He would die right before my father's eyes. Years later, when Aunt Edith was a young wife and mother, her husband would also die, leaving her to raise their four young sons. While my father stepped in to help her, she did what she could to help herself. Undaunted by unconventional work, she got a job at the nearby cemetery cleaning graves and did her job so well that she was made foreman. This early example of a woman doing what was typically a man's job left a deep impression on me. Even as a little girl I admired and respected Aunt Edith's powerful demeanor and no-nonsense personality. She knew what she wanted and did as she pleased, even to the very end. In her will, she left strict instructions to be buried on a Saturday in the white dress hanging on her closet door and in the absence of children running around and making noise.

Aunt Edna

Aunt Edith

My Father and Courage

While my aunt masked her childhood pain with her tough exterior, my father used alcohol to numb his. After my grandfather's gruesome murder, my father had no choice but to grow up fast. At only twelve, he had the responsibility of looking after his sister and stepmother. At first he resisted his demons. I know this from my mother. According to her, when she and my father were courting, he would not even drink a single beer. But over time he turned to the bottle for an outlet. While he never abused Mom or us kids, he usually became a moody, angry drunk, a transformation that tended to happen most evenings. When it did, we tried to make ourselves as invisible as possible. I would only understand the full extent of my father's personal pain decades later when I gave him a book on alcoholism. Now much older, he was finally coming to grips with his life and all that he had gone through. "Pat," he said, the tears filling his eyes, "this book is about me. I used to blame myself for my father's murder. I thought those robbers broke into the house because maybe I didn't lock the window properly that night. I told myself that I had killed him. I have carried that guilt ever since I was a boy. Alcohol was the only way for me to cope."

Despite his imperfections, I always knew that my father was a good and kind man. I was just a high school girl at Alpha Academy when that historic Hurricane Charlie slammed Kingston on August 12, 1951. I will never forget the devastation we saw as daylight broke. Buildings had been reduced to matchsticks. Entire communities had been demolished. But over the next

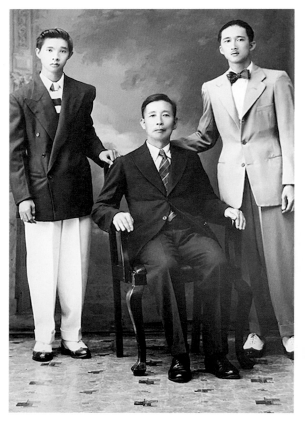

L to R: Uncle Sammy, Grandpa Charley, and Uncle Joe

Grandma Mary and Miss Pat's cousins

few weeks, I watched my father work tirelessly in our neighborhood to cut down trees, catch water, and help anyone who needed it. Thankfully, by this time, my mother had been reunited with her parents, and so we were able to help them, too. While we had always had that spirit of giving back as a family, Hurricane Charlie taught me two important lessons: one, that we should always help when possible; two, that life can change in a split second. I think that understanding made me want to make the most of my life. Time was too precious to waste.

My Dear Vincent

When I finished high school, my father encouraged me to get a bank job, something that was considered to be quite prestigious then. We were still under British rule and influence and still placing emphasis on how we dressed, spoke, and made a living.

But that rebellious streak in me was slowly awakening. I admit that I never liked conformity. In fact, I had struggled with it in school. I told my parents that I wanted to become a nurse so that I could help the sick like my idol, Mother Teresa, and promptly began a correspondence course—yesterday's equivalent of an online course—with a school in England. A year later, I ap-

Vincent "Randy" and Miss Pat (1957)

plied to the School of Nursing at the University College Hospital of the West Indies. It was while studying for my entrance exam that I met a handsome young man by the name of Vincent. The driver of my grandparents' bread van, he met me while he made a delivery next to my home. Known for skipping school and smoking marijuana, he was your typical "bad boy" and the kind of suitor no parent wanted for their daughter. To make it worse, he had fathered a child who was already a toddler. For reasons I would not understand until later into my adulthood, I was instantly attracted to him.

Rebellious Teenage Years

When I got my acceptance letter from the University College, I packed my bags to move up to the campus and into the dormitory. I jumped out of bed every morning I was enrolled in that program, eager to attend classes with my dormmates, happy about training in the ward, and proud that I was making something of my life. While the program may have felt like boot camp, that first bite into independence was as heavenly as an Oh Henry chocolate bar, my favorite candy at the time. Most of all, however, I was relieved that I was no longer under my parents' watchful eye. It meant that I could see Vincent freely. My father was not happy about this. He saw my suitor for what he was: trouble. I didn't have the self-awareness or words to express it then as a teenager, but in Vincent I sensed that familiar restlessness and pent-up energy my father had—a rage that surfaced in ways that could be creative and self-driving but also, at times, self-destructive.

For the time being, I was living my life free of intervention. Even though the dormitory had strict visitors' rules, Vincent would still make the two-hour-long bicycle ride from his home on Water Lane to visit. We were in love, and I knew he was the one for me. Midway through my studies, I became pregnant. I stayed on in school a few months longer but left when I could no longer hide the pregnancy. I was now back at home, my father so angry that he refused to speak with me. He was angry, not just because I had ruined my career plans but also because I had unknowingly repeated history—my parents had also gotten pregnant before they married. The life I thought I had been heading for was suddenly gone. But love triumphed over disappointment. A couple months later my father began speaking with me again. At that point Vincent and I got married quietly with my parents' blessing. It was a simple ceremony held in a rectory with my sister and Vincent's best friend, Wilson Hew-Fatt, acting as witnesses. Once it was over, my father returned to his trucking business, the new venture he had started just a few years before. Meanwhile, my mother cooked a nice dinner for us of curried goat, rice, and roti. There was no wedding cake, no speeches, nor photographs taken. All I have from that day is the two-foot-long piece of paper with our names on it to show that I became a wife on March 15, 1957, at the age of nineteen.

RANDYCHIN
A JAMAICAN REGGAE PIONEER
1958

Part Two

Randy's Record Mart

1957-1977

" "My Grandfather Joe would be very happy to see how Randy's Record Mart evolved into what it is today. Their business started from selling the used records out of my Granddad's jukeboxes, that Vincent helped him maintain. Vincent and Miss Pat through hard work and dedication, laid the foundation for the largest reggae recording company in the world, VP Records!"

Mr. Christopher Issa

A New Life to Start

Less than two weeks after marrying Vincent, I gave birth to our son Gregory. With Vincent no longer working for my grandparents and doing a little better for himself at a jukebox company, owned by a businessman by the name of Mr. Joseph Issa, we found a small rental apartment on Windward Road and moved in.

There we started our life as a new family with our baby and with Vincent's son, Clive, coming to visit occasionally. But just one month shy of his first birthday, Gregory took ill with meningitis and was immediately hospitalized. On the morning of his birthday, he took his last breath while I was on my way to the hospital. Distraught and five months pregnant with our second child, I heeded my doctor's advice to stay home for my health and not attend the funeral. For the sake of my well-being I was never told where my infant son was laid to rest. Four months later I gave birth to another son, Christopher. The year was 1959. I was only twenty years old, but life had already delivered some crippling blows. With faith in our hearts, we moved on.

Fortunately, Vincent was doing well at his new job. In charge of maintaining and stocking the company's jukeboxes in bars island-wide, my husband was constantly surrounded by music and loving it. Thanks to my mom who would help look after the baby, I was sometimes able to travel with Vincent

Vincent "Randy"

as he made his way around the island to service the jukeboxes, change the 45s, and collect the money. We'd drive from parish to parish making many stops between Kingston and Montego Bay, often sleeping in the car overnight. But we didn't mind. We were young and saw it as an adventure. I loved seeing people's reaction when he walked into a bar with a pile of new records. It was like watching a boxer being cheered on as he gets into the ring, or a singer as he takes the stage. Vincent got that kind of greeting. I never grew tired of seeing the joy in the eyes of the customers knowing that they were about to hear new music. That connection between music and elation stuck with me.

Soon, however, I'd see a connection of a different kind. I began to notice that Vincent would drink a beer at one or two of his stops. Because he was happy when drinking, I didn't think much of it. But the habit would continue into our years as business owners, which often meant staying at the shop way past closing time just so he could "have another" with his friends. This would anger me, particularly on the days when I was exhausted from work and needed to go home to look after our children. Looking back, I know that Vincent's troubled spirit—the reason behind his need for distraction—was rooted in his own parents' mixed-race marriage. In Vincent's case, it was his father who was Chinese, while his mother was of mixed race. His father, a prominent man in the Chinese-Jamaican society, did not interact with the

Miss Pat (Age 16)

Husband and wife, partners (1957)

Pat and baby Randy Jr. (4 months)

latter community with his non-Chinese wife. This division was something that Vincent and his siblings could not have felt good about as children. In my heart I believe that this unspoken prejudice caused my husband to develop a deep sense of insecurity, resentment, and sadness. I think that in alcohol he found a way to forget. But in music he found a way to belong.

Those were the early days of music in Jamaica, the days of those big and heavy 78 records with the gramophones that you'd have to wind up before playing the records. In those days we had mento, but it was a genre not widely appreciated or considered mainstream enough to be played on the radio. The reggae culture, of course, had not yet started. For the most part, Jamaicans listened to American R&B, gospel and country-and-western singers like Fats Domino, Elvis Presley, The Drifters, Sam Cooke, Jim Reeves, and so on. If it made us move or sing, we loved it. R&B singers felt the love when they performed in the island, which they often did. I had the pleasure of seeing stars like Little Richard, Sam Cooke, and Ray Charles at the Carib Theatre. Aretha Franklin and others also performed there. In those days we only had one local radio station. Established in 1950, RJR gave a lot of airplay to these foreign artists and very little to the local. All over the island you'd see these little boxes on the walls in bars and public places with the volume on high. This was for the benefit of the many who didn't own a radio or record player. For them, music "on demand" came through the humble jukebox.

One day, while staring at the growing pile of excess 45s Vincent had been

Kalypso Records, Jamaican record label

78 rpm Decca gramophone record

Classic
jukebox...

Where it
all started!

storing in our apartment, I thought of an idea. "Vincent," I said now turning to him, "if Mr. Issa doesn't need these old records, why don't we buy them from him and sell them direct to the public?" As soon as I said the words I saw that little girl again, peddling her marbles and rubber bands at school. Vincent stared at me with wide eyes. He was immediately sold. Things moved quickly once we agreed to strike out on our own. Vincent decided that we could call the business Randy's Record Mart after Randy Wood, the owner of a Tennessee station that Vincent used to pick up on his ham radio, and founder of Dot Records. The station, WHIN, played jazz and country music, a music genre that Vincent loved as much as R&B. Once we had our name, we went looking for a location. As luck would have it, Vincent's friend's father owned a little grocery store at the corner of East and Tower Streets that he was willing to share. So we negotiated a rental agreement for half the shop. With that, Randy's Record Mart was born in 1959. Because we decided that Vincent should keep his job until the business could comfortably support us, I ran the store while he popped in during lunchtime and then each evening when he'd pick me up to go home. Money was tight, of course, but we watched our spending and made good cash flow decisions. At this point, our goal was not to build a career in the music business per se. All we wanted to do was to make an honest living. To us—to me, at any rate—it was just a job. I could not have pictured the whirlwind life that lay ahead of us, and the joy it would bring.

40 YEARS

VP RECORDS

PATRICIA CHIN

A REGGAE MUSIC JOURNEY

ANNIVERSARY

L to R: Clive (age 9), Vincent, Pat, and Chris (age 6)

"When I started Island Records in Jamaica in 1959, there were no local records being produced other than Calypso, which sold to tourists, or Mento, which was Jamaican 'folk' music. I was one of the first to record Jamaican 'popular' music as was Eddie Seaga, who later became Prime Minister. I called on many shops that sold music. The best independent music shops were operated by the Chinese Jamaicans.... Leslie Kong, KG Records at Cross Roads, the Wong family at Wonards and Randy & Pat Chin at Randy's. The Chins built up a huge business when they moved to NYC and really became the biggest and best distributor in the U.S. of the music that was created in Jamaica."

Chris Blackwell

Moving to 17 North Parade

We were now young business owners working hard for our piece of the pie. In those days, Times Store was one of the few places in the island where you could buy American records retail. For wholesale purchases, we went to West Indies Records, the brainchild of Mr. Edward Seaga before his days as prime minister of Jamaica.

Then the owner of Jamaica's most successful record company, Mr. Seaga had the pressing and distribution rights to some American records and released records by upcoming local artists such as Byron Lee and the Dragonaires, Higgs and Wilson, and others. Still on a strict budget, I would go to Mr. Seaga's factory and buy one record at a time—and I mean literally one Fats Domino LP or maybe one Ray Charles LP—then head to Wonard's Radio Service to buy one needle, one brush, and maybe one turntable. I'd sell those items and replace the stock again and again, buying one of each until we could afford to buy in numbers. That's how Mr. Seaga and I met. I knew even then that he was a genius for seeing the potential in Jamaica's music. He would eventually enter politics and sell West Indies Records to Byron Lee, who turned it into Dynamic Sounds. Years later, when Mr. Seaga came to visit VP Records in New York, I would ask him if he remembered me. He said he did because I was his only female customer.

We were just out of the starting blocks and at least holding our heads above

Miss Pat behind the counter at Randy's Record Mart (1957)

L to R: June (Store Employee), Vincent and the late, great Millie Small

Vincent "Randy" in Studio 17

Bob Marley and the late Prime Minister,
the Most Hon. Edward Seaga

Mr. Joseph Elias Issa

45 ROOTS ROCK REGGAE

water. Offering wise advice that comes with experience, Vincent's father encouraged us to move to a better location and take Randy's to the next step. With his help, in 1961 we negotiated and secured some rental space in Charlie Moo's restaurant in the more vibrant commercial district of North Parade. I use the word "space" because that was basically what we had. At only eight-by-ten feet, our "store" was so small that if three people came in at one time, it wouldn't just be a little crowded. It would be full. As was typical of Chinese shops, we put every inch to use, covering the walls with instruments, turntable needles, and generally anything that didn't have to be stored flat. But our physical size didn't hinder our progress. With the popular Ward Theatre just across the way and some small music producers already doing business in the area, our new store at 17 North Parade immediately became a magnet for anyone in music. Singers, producers, musicians, schoolboy deejays, and even regular folks who just enjoyed music all began making Randy's a regular stop and hangout place. The relocation worked like magic. We were doing so well that within a year Vincent was able to leave his job with Mr. Issa and work full-time with me.

Thanks to a loan from my father who was doing extremely well with his trucking business, we took our next big step and bought the restaurant business and entire building from Mr. Moo. We were grateful for my father's help and belief in us as young business owners. As life would have it, he had gotten his own start as a younger man through a generous loan from Mr. Issa, the same gentlemen Vincent had worked for. The loan, based on a

Miss Pat and Vincent "Randy" Chin in Studio 17

handshake with no collateral or contract, was typical of such transactions in those days. These early examples of giving back and helping the ones behind you became our blueprint for business.

Vincent and I were now just getting into high gear. But the life of a working mother was no easier then than it is today. Having a sharp sense of organization saved me. Each evening before going to sleep, I would set the table, decide what I would make for the following day's breakfast, and prepare whatever I could ahead of time. That

kind of planning made my mornings easier when I had to get my family ready for the day and head to the shop. I think that women are gifted when it comes to multitasking—looking after our home, our children, and our work. As if I wasn't busy enough, we now had the restaurant. Even though we had downsized the menu, it still meant that we had to hit the ground running the second we got there. While serving our customers, I'd get the pot of soup going on the burner and start preparing that day's lunch selection, all of which had to be ready by eleven. It

L to R: Neville Garrick, Bunny Wailer, Bob Marley, Lee "Scratch" Perry, Skill Cole, and Dennis Thompson (Engineer) at the Dream Concert rehearsal

Record stamper machine at Randy's Studio 17

was crazy work but we were young and still learning about business and what it took to generate a strong cash flow. For a while, keeping the food side of the business made sense. Customers who came to shop would sometimes grab a patty and a soda or soup for lunch. It was an odd combination, but it helped to give us a little edge. I still remember this American fellow from New York who used to travel the Caribbean selling American records. He would always come by Randy's on his Jamaica stops. "Miss Pat," he said one day as I handed him his patty. "I have seen many record stores in my lifetime. But never have I seen one with a restaurant in it!"

Still doing well with our current business formula, we nevertheless remained open-minded to new possibilities. Not long after buying the building we expanded the store, closed the restaurant, and replaced it with an automobile accessories section for better profitability. The new market demand for fuzzy dice, scented car hangers, floor mats, and the like was a craze we could not ignore. Before long, our automotive accessories department carried pots and pans and other miscellaneous items that were in high demand. That's how we Chinese were, though—hardwired for business. If it sold, we carried it. The decision proved to be a good one. In no short order we bought the building next door and began construction on our next significant step: our own studio. In those days, there was no one-stop studio where one could complete their work from start to finish. Back then you had to go to one place to do a recording and then another to do the mastering. With more and more artists and producers emerging and with the

Yellowman outside of Randy's Record Mart

existing studios charging high fees, we designed the studio to be a full house production studio so that we could be completely independent. Bill Garnet, who passed away maybe twenty years ago, helped to set up the studio for us. He got the main parts we needed, like a disc cutter to cut the vinyl and a stamper to master the records, while Vincent brought back a cut and lathe from the States, as well as a stock of needles, turntable mats, and anything to do with recording. Before long, our studio was operational. All we needed was a name. This time we kept it simple: Studio 17.

Randy's Record Mart—shoppers
Chris Chin (Age 7), his Dad Vincent and shoppers

Take your pick from
Randy's
parade of top hits

"There is a small street, more like an alley, with a few parked cars and bikes and a dozen or so guys, dreads, leaning against the wall on the shady side. This is the legendary 'Idler's Rest,' next to Randy's Record Shop. It's where musicians, singers and hangers-on get together every day. It functions as a private office, employment agency, public relations agency and talent show for many singers and studio musicians and young upstarts looking for a place in the music business. Next door, at Randy's Record Shop, they're spinning the new 45's. The sound, blending with the street noise, flows around the corner."

TED BAFALOUKOS

Studio 17 and Idler's Rest

If location is the door then timing is the key that opens it. Vincent and I had unknowingly caught the wave of an industry that was just beginning to swell. At this point, ska was still struggling for local recognition. Radio DJs almost never played it on the air, not even when a second radio station—Jamaica Broadcasting Corporation ("JBC")—joined the airwaves in 1959.

But that would change as the country headed toward independence from England in 1962. Hearing Jamaican music being played for the first time on radio would be a breakthrough moment for a nation coming into its own and increasingly enjoying self-expression through song. It was a mood that Vincent sensed instinctively. One of the first local artists that Vincent produced was the calypso singer Lord Creator, who originally hailed from Trinidad and Tobago. When Vincent ran into the singer at the Havana Nightclub in Kingston, he asked him if he would record a song about Jamaica's upcoming independence. Lord Creator agreed and "Independent Jamaica" went on to become a hit. At first the radio stations resisted playing it, but with people everywhere singing the lyrics, the radio stations eventually gave the people what they wanted and gave the song airplay. One month after Independence in August of 1962, I gave birth to another son. We were so busy that we hadn't yet thought of a name for him, so I decided to keep it simple and name him Vincent, after his father. And because we needed a

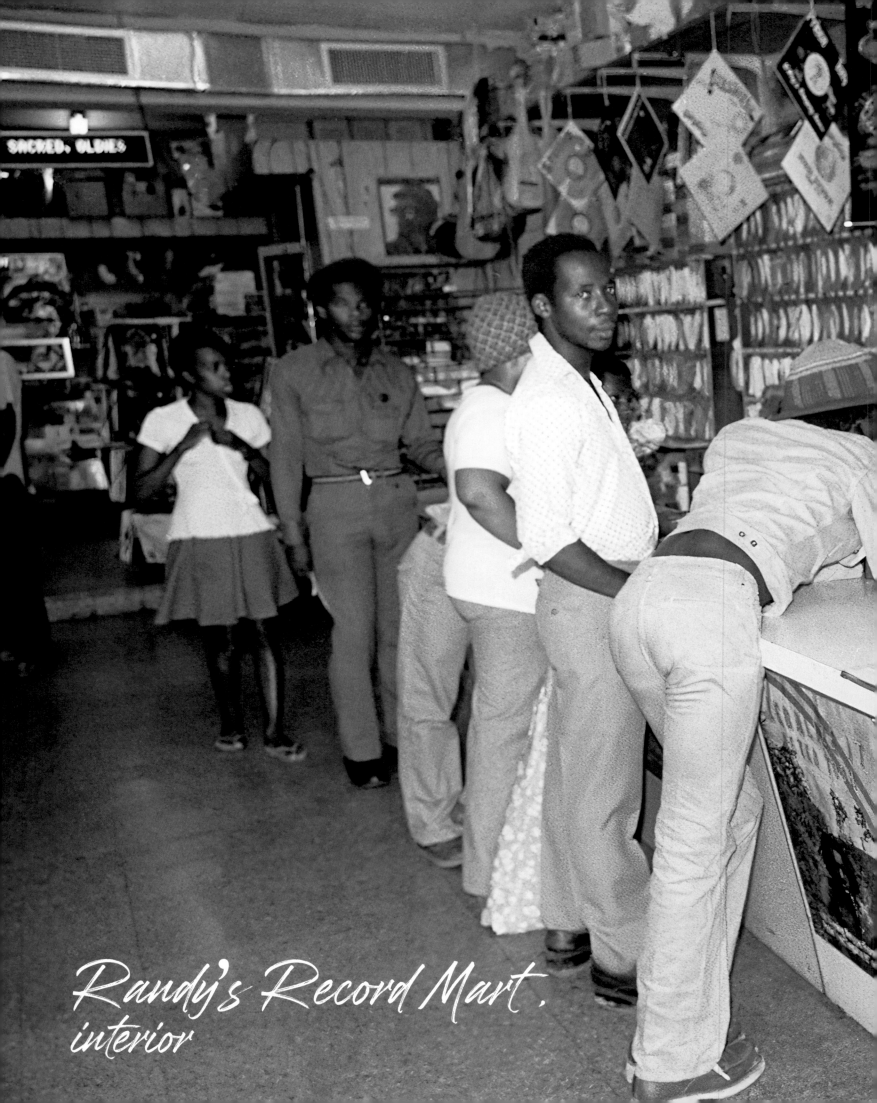

Randy's Record Mart, interior

Angela Chin (age 12) at Randy's Record Mart

met Gerry Mulligan and Sonny Stitt. He would also go on to meet the likes of Fats Domino and Johnny Nash. Nash, of "I Can See Clearly Now" fame, would end up doing many recordings in Jamaica, making him, it is said, the first non-Jamaican artist to record reggae on the island. When Vincent invited Nash, his manager Danny Sims, and arranger Arthur Jenkins to Studio 17 while on one of their visits to Jamaica, the singer loved it so much that he booked it for three months straight.

After that, Studio 17 itself became a hit, signaling to us that it was time to open it up to the industry for bookings. Not only did everyone want to record there, all the artists would come just to socialize, a huge convenience for whoever was up in the studio working. For instance, if the recording artist needed an extra backup singer, they'd pop their head downstairs, see who was available, and say, "Delroy Wilson! Come up here and do a backing." Or, "Come on, Keith Poppin, come up here and sing this chorus for us!" If the artists were available for hire, they would sign a contract on a little piece of paper and head upstairs. That was how it was done then—on the spot and informally. We'd open the studio from nine in the morning and start bookings by ten. This is when Randy's and Studio 17 really became this fantastic "enjoyment agency." It was roughly at this time that I began to hear our little part of North Parade being referred to as "Idler's Rest." I can't recall the exact moment when I first heard it, but I remember smiling. It was a perfect name. On Saturdays, our store was always packed with people of all sorts—people from sound systems, shopkeepers from the country areas,

middle name we chose Randy, after the business. Now busier than ever with a growing family and expanding business, I turned to my mother again for help with my new baby.

With Studio 17 now producing music in this exciting period, we were confident that our investment would pay off. Thankfully for us, things just happened naturally as we grew from stage to stage, from selling records retail, to selling wholesale, to producing and distributing. This kept us hopping and forced Vincent to do a lot of traveling. On his trips to the States for supplies, he would try to stay current with the music genres there, and occasionally popped into jazz clubs. This is how he and even visitors from abroad. They'd fill our store and spill over onto the sidewalk, happy to just be hearing the music, seeing friends, and soaking up the vibe. They all came because of the music. Even today, people will tell me how they would skip school or come by right after, just to hear the music and be part of that creative mood. "Miss Pat," they'll say, "I used to come to the shop as a little bwoy when you were selling records back on North Parade. Me is ole man now but you still here! How yuh still so young?" I'll laugh and tell them the truth. "I don't honestly know...maybe it's the music that keeps me young." Sometimes the schoolboys who came to the shop couldn't afford to buy anything. And if they did buy something, the money they spent was most likely their lunch money. I guess some of them preferred to spend the little money they had on music instead of food. They wanted nourishment for the soul over nourishment for the body. I couldn't blame them. The music of those days took you to a different level. It had the power to give you the same feeling you have when you're in love.

Tommy McCook and Dirty Harry

Idler's Rest. Alley behind Randy's Record Shop. Kingston. Eric Clarke. Horsemouth. & Bongo Herman. Dec 1976

" "I started working at Randy's Records as a kid moving boxes at my parents' store. And one of the first memories I have is of meeting Lord Creator when I was seven years old. Jamaica's creativity comes from its cultural diversity—it is home to people from different roots, from East Indian to Chinese to African and more. I think VP has been so successful because there is a genuine love for the music and the sense of belonging to the history of reggae and its heritage."

Christopher Chin

This Is Ska

The sixties was an incredibly exciting time for music in Jamaica, and Randy's was right in the middle of that party. By this time, Jamaican radio DJs started playing local music more often. Encouraged by the trend, Vincent pushed to get artists to record their songs in his studio at night, after which he would try to get the records played the very next day. We scored early hits this way with Basil Gabbidon, Jackie Opel, and Toots and the Maytals. Lord Creator's "We Will Be Lovers" also became another big hit.

Those early songs have not lost their appeal or significance. When I went to the Rototom Reggae Sunsplash in Benicàssim, Spain, in 2014, the British radio DJ and disc jockey David Rodigan was at the controls. For almost the entire time I was there, the world-renowned reggae aficionado saluted our family by playing Vincent's earlier productions like "Independent Jamaica" and "Don't Stay Out Late." Tears flooded my eyes when it occurred to me that most of the fans there dancing and singing weren't even a thought in their parents' minds when that music was being produced. Then, just as we were making our way through the crowd to find something to eat, one of our songs with Lord Creator came blasting through the speakers. The crowd went crazy. "Oh my God," I said to myself, "that record wasn't even a hit in Jamaica!"

Witnessing the Early Struggles

I feel blessed for having been there in the early days of seeing and being a part of the struggle to give Jamaican

Storefront of Randy's Record Mart –
Uncle Herbert and Randy Chin Jr. (age 12) admiring a motorbike

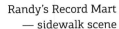
music a chance. Many of those first musicians didn't even have the money for proper instruments. Oftentimes they made their own instruments like drumsticks, drums, and stringed instruments. Because we believed in the music and their talent, we helped when we could. I remember Courtney Panton coming into our store and looking at some of the instruments on display. Only sixteen or seventeen at the time, he started staring at this one guitar as if it was a beautiful girl. I could see in his eyes that he really wanted it. But when he admitted he didn't have all the money for it, I said, "OK, how much yuh have?" I ended up selling him the guitar, of course. Charlie Organaire, who would go on to become a great musician, got his harmonica from us that way when he was even younger. As I did with the others, I told him he could pay us back gradually. Sometimes the musicians would honor their end of the deal, sometimes they didn't. But we took our chances because we saw the value in these youngsters learning a craft and making something of themselves. I have no regrets. In most cases, it worked out.

But that was our life—living among the early musicians in the early stages of their careers when we all were young and full of hope and dreams.

Vincent was very sociable so they all gravitated towards him. The musicians would hang out by the store, laughing and joking and talking about music. People like Tommy McCook, Roland Alphonso, Lester Sterling, and Don Drummond would be there, as well as Rico Rodriguez before he left for England. Johnny "Dizzy" Moore, one of Jamaica's best trumpeters from even back then, was another familiar face in our store. Usually barefoot, he'd spend hours talking

with Vincent and playing the trumpet, with Vincent joining him on his own trumpet. (Many of these earlier musicians, especially the talented ones, got their foundation training at the Alpha Boys School, which is why the Vincent and Patricia Foundation continues to engage in charity work with the school.) Vincent was also close to the Rastafarian movement and would often go visit the Rastafarians in the hills where he'd stay for hours drumming and chanting with them.

Sound of Jamaica Enters the World Stage

Life was moving at a nice even clip for us. But there was more in store. As we rang in 1964, no one could have predicted that this would be the breakout year for Jamaican music. That was the year Byron Lee took his band, along with a young Jimmy Cliff and Prince Buster, to the World's Fair in New York to promote Jamaica's ska music and dance. Only a month before, Chris Blackwell's Island Records had released Millie Small's version of "My Boy Lollipop," which ended up being a huge hit in England and the first big break for Blackwell. When he brought Millie Small to our store to meet us that summer, I remember marveling to myself that the singing sensation looked like she was only fifteen or sixteen. But she would go down in history as being the first female Jamaican artist to put Jamaican music

Prince Buster

on the charts. As a woman in what was mostly a man's industry, I felt an extra level of pride about Small's huge achievement. So when just two months later in September I gave birth to our daughter, Angela, I felt comforted knowing that the women who came before her were already shattering that glass ceiling. Those were the glory days of our youth, when we drove ourselves on energy and dreams. Those were the days when a young Chris Blackwell used to literally carry Bob Marley 45s under his arm trying to sell them, long before Bob became a superstar. I still laugh when I think back to how incredibly naïve we all were as we went about doing our thing. We were riding on pure faith.

It has to be said that Vincent and I worked well together as a team even in those early days when we were still figuring things out. As a woman, I felt blessed to have a husband who trusted my business instincts. From the moment we opened shop selling those excess 45s, we ran the business as equal partners. The division of duties also played to our strengths, something that benefited the business. With me in the store full-time, Vincent was free to fly to the States to buy American records, get whatever inventory the store needed, and do business with the industry players abroad. One day, he took a chance and brought back a few copies of a new song by a Trinidadian singer produced under an American label. The song was "Shame and Scandal (In the Family)." Not long after Vincent returned to Jamaica, the sound systems turned the song into an instant hit. Vincent didn't hesi-

tate. He practically jumped on the next flight back to the States, this time to buy one thousand copies. To give ourselves a head start over the competition, we scratched off the labels so no one would know the name and sold it at the higher prerelease price before anyone could catch on. We made a lot of money that way. The other record stores didn't know the singer, producer—nothing! And boy did Jamaicans find that song irresistible with its humorous lyrics. Peter Tosh also did a version of that song. As a people, we appreciate comedy and don't hesitate to blend it with music. Vincent even recorded the comedy act Bim and Bam, and may have been the first label to do so.

"Studio 17 was the main studio in the early '70s because that was one of the first independents, before even Channel One. All the producers were going there, and most of the reggae producers have recorded there. When I did my first sessions, it was twenty dollars an hour, so I could rent the studio for three hours and pay my musicians and work on songs. Randy's was the studio at the time. A lot of hits came out of there. And Miss Pat was there every day."

Twinkle Brothers / Norman Grant

Rocksteady

In 1966, a new sound by the name of rocksteady entered the stage. As the music changed so did the dance, which is why we never got bored with the industry. Even then, dancing was one of Jamaica's biggest forms of entertainment, particularly as the average person downtown didn't have money for movies or holidays.

Organized dances were the closest form of entertainment for them. These took place in what was called a "yard," which was essentially a piece of ground surrounded by a zinc fence. The promoters would put up their equipment with the big speaker boxes and let people enter and dance or stand outside if they wanted to just chat and make jokes and just enjoy themselves. At the time we didn't appreciate how unique those simple but energetic gatherings were, especially for the young. It was a beautiful time for creativity, too, because sound systems weren't just about singers and deejays. It was a starting ground for many different careers. Thanks to these dances, a young carpenter could find work building the speaker boxes, while an apprentice electrician could handle the wiring.

Sound Systems

You could really feel the energy that drove the industry forward. And it wasn't just about new job opportunities. Music tapped into your creativity no matter your skill or line of business.

Take the sound systems, for instance. People would follow their favorites, such as Duke Reid, Prince Buster, and Coxsone wherever they played. It was pure entertainment. You'd have Count Machuki and King Stitt on the mic, hyping the records and "cursing" at each other. But even though they were competing, they brought communities together and gave them a sense of belonging because they were challenging each other with words and songs, not guns. It was

healthy, vibrant, uplifting, and just plain exciting like fighters in a boxing ring. This is why we have to give credit to those sound systems. When in the early days you couldn't get your records played on radio, it was the sound systems that showed us what the people liked and what they didn't. You could see the reaction at the dances and how people gravitated to the music and the beat. That was the only way we could know what was a hit.

It was for this reason that most producers had sound systems. In addition to being a good testing ground, a sound system gave a producer a way to advertise their music. Sometimes they would get a new "riddim" (rhythm) fresh from the studios and play the dubplate right there, or have an artist like Dennis Brown come by to sing over it. Those sound systems had a good thing going. And let's not forget the deejays. They were a vital part of the culture, too, because each time the music was playing, they'd be toasting and rhyming over the riddims and basically creating something new and original each time. They knew how to really energize a crowd. The dances became like therapy—people would go there, spend two or three hours enjoying themselves and forgetting their troubles. It's not that you don't have them anymore but you leave with a new perspective. You have a different handle on your situation. If you had a grievance with someone before going to the dance, it's possible you could leave seeing it differently because of the music. The Chinese, as a community, played a significant role in this sound system culture, something that I was always quite proud of as a Chinese Jamaican. Because the Chinese had their small grocery businesses scattered all over the island, their shops usually became the natural gathering point of most communities—an early "distribution" point if you will for anyone wishing to spread news, messages, and trends. And because the Chinese were usually—although not always—the ones with a little money, they could afford to invest in the sound system equipment. In this way they helped with the development of music. And it is for this reason their shops became a natural hub for politicians. Even today, sound systems are part of the political arena and a popular way to gather a crowd and for the politician to deliver a particular message. To date, Jamaica has had two prime ministers with strong connections to the music industry. Mr. Seaga was involved on the production and distribution side, while Mr. P.J. Patterson focused on the legal aspects. Many people marvel at the number of Chinese who got involved with

Jamaican music. But I believe this connection between the grocery shop and the sound system culture is how several Chinese-Jamaicans—such as Leslie Kong and Byron and Neville Lee—became enchanted by the island's most famous calling card.

Duke Reid

"Once a friend loaned Horace Swaby a plastic melodica, a handheld keyboard instrument normally used to teach children the rudiments of music, the ethereal songs he conjured on it under the alias of Augustus Pablo ushered in a whole new era at Randy's. The wonderful 'Java' is a pioneering work that straddles the realms of straightforward instrumentals and more complex dub works, being a stunning example of all that the studio was capable of at that time."

Edward Seaga

Keeping My Ear to the Street

As the music grew more and more fascinating, so did my appreciation and genuine love for it. I particularly enjoyed the humor in some of those records as well. Some like Prince Buster could be potentially controversial. He did songs like "Black Head Chinaman," a song that would prompt harmless chuckling in the Caribbean, but raise eyebrows elsewhere. In the spirit of playful bantering, something that Caribbean people are known for, Prince Buster and Derrick Morgan would even sing songs about each other.

I was always interested in how the lyrics translated their feelings. While it was never usually about anything too serious, you did have the occasional fuss. Take Prince Buster and Beverley's, for instance. They had a little tension going on because Derrick Morgan used to sing for Prince Buster before going to Beverley's, so there was a war of words between them through lyrics. In many ways the music was like a newspaper—and even our pre-Internet social media. You could learn what was going on in the country just by listening to the music. Sometimes the messages were strong ones—like "Why don't you put away your guns?" And, of course, sometimes they were just a whole lot of fun.

Meanwhile, the industry continued to challenge my skills as a businesswoman as well as my knowledge of music. Determined to stay at the top of my game, I sharpened my skills with on-the-job practice. For instance, the prerelease of 45s was a supply-and-demand practice that kept me busy with our bookkeeping. Typically, the 45s would be sold first at the higher prerelease price for two to

Randy's Record Mart – vendors

three weeks to the sound system guys. They had one goal in mind: to have the best and most recent releases. Once the competition with their rivals was over, we would drop the price for the general public. As I said, there was a whole lot of bookkeeping going on at that counter of mine. I also had to be quick on my feet—literally. Sales could really get hectic at Randy's when the music was being played. Customers would hear it and rush the counter wanting to buy ten or so. I developed and honed my A&R skills from behind the counter at Randy's, where I would play test pressings from our upstairs Studio 17, in order to gauge customers' reactions. This interaction with my customers helped me to decide which tracks to release. I also had to be a walking encyclopedia of music. Sometimes customers would come in without knowing the name of a song they had in mind. "Mi want some music but mi nuh know di name a di tune, Miss Pat." But that never stumped me. "Hum it for me," I'd tell them. Without fail I would find the song. This happened with the famous selector Tony Screw—a.k.a. Downbeat The Ruler—who came in one day looking for a specific remix of John Holt's "Stick By Me" hit. "Mi check all di stores uptown and downtown," he said, "and walk all over Orange Street. But dem eedah don't have it or don't know it!" He really needed it, he said, for an upcoming clash. The problem was, because the labels had been scratched off, he didn't know the song's name. So I told him to hum it for me. After a few minutes of searching, I handed him the elusive record with a huge smile, happy that I had found it. "Here it is!" He was so thrilled he burst out laughing. "Miss Pat! Miss Pat, yuh di don! If anyone else comes in here asking for it, tell dem yuh don't have it."

The Producers

As we evolved in the industry, my ear became sharper. Just as I had learned something new, the record producers would come up with new ideas and sounds. But that didn't deter me. I soon learned to tell the different labels apart just from the sound, without even seeing the label itself. Let me tell you—I was having a blast and seizing every opportunity to learn as much as I could from anyone who would teach me. Duke Reid was one of those who entertained all my questions. He was someone I rated highly, as evidenced from the amount of his records we used to buy from him for our shop. I never did meet him in person, but we'd have long conversations on the phone about music and the music business. An ex-policeman who had a haberdashery and liquor store with a studio above it, his persona was large. I never saw this for myself, but rumor had it that he would wear a crown on his head and let fans carry him into the dancehall on their shoulders. From his pictures I could tell that he was a large man, which may have been the reason some people feared him, especially given the fact that he did business in rough areas. But I thought he was just a really nice person, and recording artists in general felt that he treated them fairly. I also consider Duke Reid and Coxsone Dodd of Studio One to be among Jamaica's greatest producers. Proof is the fact that their songs are being played even today. They took a chance on young artists at a time when it was risky, risky because we didn't really have something called Jamaican music. Without pioneering producers like these, we wouldn't be here today. Their vision and passion helped to give the country its own musical legacy.

Despite the heavy competition, the producers, artists, dancers and deejays each had their time on the spinning wheel of fame. We saw it for ourselves. That part of Kingston where we were located on North Parade became a haven for record stores and all things music. Everything you needed was right there, whether it was a record, musical instrument, studio, or pressing plant. We were a community—a melting pot of sound and talent. Across the street from us was Charlie's Record, the famous portable snow cone cart record shop, while producer Joe Gibbs was next door to us. In the same radius for three to four blocks you had the Techniques, Beverley's, Prince Buster, Tip Top Records, Duke Reid, Coxsone, and a few others. Those were the days when just about every singer and producer had a little retail store where they could sell their own records.

L to R: Dennis Thompson, Errol Thompson, Clive Chin, & Augustus Pablo

Foreigners Begin to Take Note

It was around this time that foreigners began to take serious interest in Jamaican music, even going as far as traveling regularly to the island. When they did, they would flock to Idler's Rest so they could buy records or sign up new artists. I remember Lee Gopthal of Trojan Records in the UK being one of those who would fly in fairly often to do just that. He knew what records were hot and doing well. He would drop by in front of our store to meet with the producers, talk a bit, pay them, and leave.

And he wasn't the only one. With England being the biggest market for Jamaican music at that time, you'd often see British record company representatives, producers, and vendors standing out on the sidewalk in front of Randy's signing up whomever they could and making deals with the players in the industry. With our wide front door always open, I could quite literally watch the negotiations taking place from where I stood behind the counter. I don't think that any of us saw the role of Idler's Rest then for what it really was: the unofficial epicenter of

Jamaican music. All we knew was that magic was happening—and happening every day.

By this time I had reconnected with my old Greenwich Farm neighbor, Bunny Lee, now a young music producer coming up strong in the industry. I still remember when he wanted to record a song called "Wet Dream." The problem was that none of the artists wanted to sing on it because they felt the name was too suggestive. But Bunny was always thinking out of the box that way. Finally, Max Romeo agreed to do it. And the song no one wanted to sing became a Top 10 hit in England. In fact, it spent nearly 20 weeks on the British charts. "Boy, I wish I had trusted Bunny," was all you could hear from the other artists after that. On the heels of "Wet Dream," Bunny teamed up with Eric Donaldson to do "Cherry Oh Baby," which scored another win for him.

Bunny Lee

Tuning Into the One-Stop Approach

But it was rough for all the producers starting out at a time when only a few could see their vision. Back then, the very small producers were forced to walk around with their box of records, selling here and there. That was their only option. One day, I decided to convince them to leave the records at Randy's on consignment. I was the first one to give them a book and say, "Just leave me what you want, write the number down here, and when you return I'll pay you for what I sold and give back the rest." Naturally, we added enough to the price of the record to make a profit for our work. This arrangement saved people the hassle of having to go to five different places to buy what they wanted and put us in the position to see what sold and what didn't. And it could really be sad at times. We'd see these young singers bringing in their new tracks, trying desperately to turn it into a hit, but not always seeing it happen. At times your heart ached when you saw their faces drenched in disappointment. You wanted so much for their dreams to come true. This decision to sell everyone's music is how the wholesale part of our business came about. I made sure we had at least one of every artist's records because, for us, it was all about the customer. So even though Joe Gibbs refused to sell to us because we were right next door to each other, I would simply get someone else to buy us a few copies for our inventory. I got that one-stop concept from my parents' and grandparents' shopkeeper training, of course. Even if we made only one red cent on it, we were determined to live up to the slogan emblazoned on

our Randy's sign outside: You Name It, We Have It. Honestly, I don't remember a single day when I didn't want to jump out of bed and head straight to the shop.

As is the case with all business partners, Vincent and I didn't always agree on everything. For instance, we were the only producers without our own sound system. I used to fuss and complain that it would have given us an edge, but the truth was the store itself was our substitute sound system and source of feedback. After finishing a recording upstairs, Vincent would put the song on a disc and literally run downstairs to play it in the shop for all to hear. It was instant gratification—cutting and recording the tracks, then playing it for an eager test audience. From their reaction, we could tell if something was going to be a hit or not. I also used to question Vincent about the kinds of records he was making. Because I was the one behind the counter, I knew what was selling. "Maybe we should make records like Coxsone does," I'd suggest. "Or Duke Reid." Or, "Why are you making all this soft music?" But it simply wasn't in his DNA. As I look back, I see now that Vincent was using the studio in a different way. He was using it to help teach the young musicians how to record music. And I'm so glad he did.

"When I think about Miss Pat and Vincent Chin of Randy's Records, I know that Randy's was everybody's friend, Randy's Records come in the business and help a lot of people who couldn't get rich anywhere, and Vincent, he was one of the best man in Jamaica; him help us all.

Before they set up the studio, they did find a likkle shop down in Parade, and then they were selling so much records. So that's where Joe Gibbs go set up after him find out that Randy's was down there and they were selling so much. Randy was the first person who was setting up something for people to survive, so they were the best people in the record business. They were simply the best, and Miss Pat was the brain—she is the brain. The woman is the brain. And Randy is a man who was very friendly, but Miss Pat was behind him, the wife."

Lee "Scratch" Perry

Studio 17:
Dub
Organizers

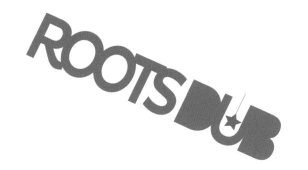

With demand for Studio 17 soaring, we ran a tight ship. I was the one who took the bookings—name of customer and time—while our manager, "CB," made sure we stuck to the schedule.

It was through the bookings that I learned that Winston "Niney" Holness was another person who believed in efficiency. This man only ever booked one hour at a time and yet came out with many hits.

One day, Vincent went up to him. "Niney," he said, "is how you produce all these hits in so short a time? What's your secret?" Niney replied, "Vincent, let me tell you something. I rehearse my songs in my house a thousand times before setting one toe in your studio. I do that because I have only enough money to buy one hour of studio time."

I used to love hearing those stories from Vincent. Even though I was at Randy's six days a week, I was usually so busy running the shop floor that I didn't have time to go into the studio, even though I really wanted to. But I didn't mind; that 20-foot-long counter was my universe and my classroom. Not only did I handle the money, I interacted with our customers and knew each one's taste like a true salesperson. I advised them on music based on whether they were an uptowner or downtowner, and the type of crowd they played for. It got tricky, too, because many of the sound system guys would come in to buy the latest record and assume that they were the only ones to get the copy. We'd " lowe dem,"

as we say in Jamaica and let them think that. This need to be first and different was the reason many made one-off dubplates for themselves. By slightly altering a record so that it had more bass, for instance, or a different word here and there, each sound system was guaranteed to be the only one with that unique version. This customization helped to give birth to the dubplate phenomenon, that sound system operators practice to this day. All this creativity meant more business for Studio 17. Raw talent—it was the pulse and heartbeat of those early reggae days.

The energy level at Randy's always shot up whenever producers—especially the big ones—walked in. Sometimes they had their little feuds, but they usually patched it up with humor. Vincent loved interacting with them any chance he could. "What kind of rhythm you making today, sir?" he would ask Lee "Scratch" Perry. Perry, to the delight of the customers, would usually reply by saying that he was going to "mash up the studio," in reference to the reputation he had for creating new sounds that were ahead of their time. Even in those days he was known for using anything from tin cans to walking sticks to hitting two pieces of wood together. He knew what he wanted to express and did it his way. As Bunny Lee used to say, "Any spoil can become a style." Indeed, it was often the case that a mistake made in the studio would be left in the song if it sounded good. But from day one, Lee Perry was in his own league, even just from the way he dressed and acted. It's no wonder he went on to become one of the originators of dub and someone who helped to shape the sound of Jamaican music today. Many people called him

a madman, but he didn't care. He was bold that way. Nowadays it's more acceptable to go against the grain, but in those days it required courage.

A Young Man Called Bob

Vincent loved Lee Perry. We saw a lot of him because he was one of those producers who would book our studio for a month at a time and practically live up there. This was the case when he was working on early Bob Marley and the Wailers songs. Their albums Soul Rebels and Soul Revolution were recorded at Studio 17, as well as some of the Wailers' early self-productions like "Lively Up Yourself" and "Trench Town Rock." At that time, Bob Marley was just another singer and not seen as anyone special, but Lee Perry's ear for a different kind of sound helped to set Bob on his way to fame. In fact, when Bob first started coming around to Randy's at fifteen or sixteen, we didn't even know he was an artist. We knew he sang with a couple other guys, but because he was so quiet we didn't know that much about him. Oftentimes he'd come in only to look for his friend Allan "Skill" Cole so they could go play ball. Peter Tosh was another quiet one who didn't socialize much either. He was very stern and businesslike. Always punctual, he would usually head straight upstairs when he had the studio. And when he was finished his work, he would just leave.

We also did a few early recordings with The Wailers, but were a little late riding that wave because it coincided with Bob's first few hits abroad. By this time his fame in Jamaica was on the rise, with some people now calling him a superstar. Jamaicans all over took note as

A young Bob Marley and Skill Cole

Lee "Scratch" Perry
in studio

Bob's newfound fame took hold abroad. Meanwhile, back at Randy's we were suddenly scrambling to pull out of storage all the old Bob Marley records that had not sold before. With customers now clamoring to buy them, we were literally pulling them out from under the counter, dusting them off, and selling them. We couldn't stop marveling at how things had changed. By this time Bob had also changed his appearance by growing his famous dreadlocks. That alone was different—and bold. To be Rasta in those early days was not something that would bring you acceptance because of the stigma of it being unclean. It would take some time before Jamaica on a whole accepted his music—even the radio stations resisted at first—but no one could deny that he was instrumental in bringing to light the struggles of the poor.

From our vantage point, we could tell that Bob had a good attitude, which no doubt helped lead him to success. Determined to grow, he listened to Chris Blackwell's guidance and worked hard on his career. A good attitude is something I have always believed in as a business owner. Other than working hard, you have to be willing to accept the fact that you have to lay the groundwork before the money comes. I believe in this as much as I believe in ethics. You must do whatever you can to the best of your ability, and receive an honest day's pay for an honest day's work. I also believe in teaching people new skills. For example, if someone came in to sweep, I would expect them to do a good job. And if they did, then I would teach them to do something else to see what their natural abilities were. It didn't matter what it was— filing, stocktaking or anything else. I would encourage them to branch out and try something new. After all, the more we achieve, the better we feel about ourselves. Loyalty is also important. We have people working with us today who were with us from our days at North Parade. Without loyal employees and customers you won't achieve much. The customers, in particular, will tell you when you're doing well or not. I see all these elements—together with having a good product—as being the ingredients of business success.

Christmastime

In those vibrant downtown Kingston days, time was like a video machine on fast-forward speed. It was even more energetic at Christmastime when we used to stay open for literally 24 hours without a thought to closing. From Christmas Eve to Christmas morning, people would come to buy music and celebrate in the streets. It was safe then and we weren't afraid to stay downtown. But even outside of the holiday season, Idler's Rest knew no rest. Each morning we pulled up to the store there'd be a small crowd of people congregating outside and waiting for us to raise our roller shutters. Some were customers but others were vendors—of fruits and other items—who sold their goods on the sidewalk. To help them out, we'd let them store their goods overnight in our shop for safekeeping. We were like one big community looking out for one another. This natural wish to help each other would become even more important as the political situation grew increasingly restless, an issue that encouraged some Jamaicans to make a new life abroad.

Keith Comes Home

Vincent's brother Keith was one of those who had left for America long before things got bad. But when his health began to suffer, Vincent made him an offer. "Why don't you come back home to recuperate? You could help me in the studio." Once Keith accepted his brother's offer there was no looking back. While Jamaica rejuvenated Keith, Keith added another dimension to the recording arm of our business. Suddenly there he was making all these hits upstairs in Studio 17 and bubbling over with life. Every time he made a record he'd come running down the stairs. "Pat! Pat, I have a hit!" He took his upbeat nature and made instant connections with everyone, such as Niney, Bunny Lee, and Lee Perry. Keith was just this energetic person who saw excitement in everything he did, even if it was a simple game of dominoes. He'd be the loudest bigmouth at the table, running jokes and making everyone laugh. That was his way.

Keith was now part of the business. With his style of music being different from the kind that we had been making before, we launched the Impact label. His was the kind of music I had been encouraging Vincent to make all along—the kind that people wanted to hear at a dance, and the kind that could compete with songs produced by the likes of Dennis Brown, Gregory

Jack Ruby

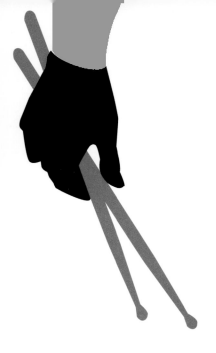

Isaacs, Alton Ellis, and Jimmy London. We weren't the only ones to have multiple labels. By then, many producers were operating under various labels because they didn't want their customers to know that all the different records were coming from the same source. It was a move I completely agreed with. Car manufacturers had long been using this tactic. In the end, we would have about twenty labels, each with different types of songs and sounds.

Next Generation, First Steps

Things, they say, happen for a reason. With our new Impact label now making waves, the seventies were proving to be an even busier and more prolific decade for us. That's when we produced hits like "Don't Go" by Horace Andy, "Lonely Soldier" by Gregory Isaacs, and "Java" by a young Augustus Pablo who was still in his teens at the time of its release. (He played his melodica on that one.) Produced by my stepson, Clive, who had come to live with us when he turned fifteen, "Java" was a big hit and an instant classic that won the Instrumental of the Year award in 1972. It basically launched Augustus' solo career and showcased Clive's talent as a producer. After having grown up in the music industry and watching it develop from the ground up, Clive's intelligence and musical intuition was put to good use. Errol Thompson, who did the mixing and engineering for us, was an old classmate of his and another musical talent who did his part to advance the music. While Clive was trying out his skills as a young producer, his younger brother Chris had already made his debut at the store

as an all-rounder. He was only seven when he started coming to the store, but immediately took to the bustling atmosphere and mixed bag of tasks he had to do. From stocking the shelves to selling and checking the money, he threw himself into Randy's like it was a candy store. Randy and Angela would also begin their "internship" when they were even younger. It was good for the kids, not just to learn life skills, but also to get a taste for the family business. I still see the North Parade chapter of our life as the glory days—a time when we were raising our children and our business together.

Behind the Hits

Meanwhile, we continued along not knowing what the next day would bring. This was especially true when it came to hits. We never saw our biggest one coming, period. Carl Malcolm's "Fattie Bum-Bum" had only been—at best—a fair seller in Jamaica. As catchy as it was, it couldn't compete with records by Dennis Brown and Gregory Isaacs. Not long after its release, however, we started getting multiple calls from England asking for licensing permission. It turned out that the kids in England simply loved it. Plans were made for Carl to perform there. But when he arrived, he got stage fright. In fairness, he was in new territory. He had never performed live on a huge stage before with no backup, no singers, no chorus, nothing. But in those days, Jamaican artists weren't trained in the art of live performance or taught how to speak or dress or handle interviews professionally. We were so naïve about these things. But then again we never dreamt of having an artist with a hit record in England.

Dennis Brown was another artist who delivered hit after hit in the seventies for Niney. Not only was Niney a great producer, he was a serious one. I'll never forget the story he told me behind "Cassandra." According to Niney, right in the middle of producing the song, Dennis came down with pneumonia and ended up being hospitalized. Desperate to have the singer voice "Cassandra," Niney sneaked him out of the hospital for a few hours one night just so he could finish the recording. Also dedicated to his music, Dennis was one of those artists who did everything from the heart and with great humility. Alton Ellis, in my opinion, was a lot like this. In 2008, when word got out that he was losing his fight with cancer, I called and spoke to him from where he lay in his hospital bed in West London's Hammersmith Hospital. When he answered I barely recognized his voice; he was so weak. Still, he mustered the energy to take a short walk down memory lane with me. "Miss Pat," he said, "do you remember down at North Parade when I made 'Too Late to Turn Back Now'?" That was almost forty years back in time and yet to him it was as if he was right back in Studio 17. I swore I could almost hear the smile return to his face. Fighting back the tears for his sake, I told him that he was a great artist and that he and his songs would never be forgotten. "Alton," I said, "your son Christopher is making music now. Your voice will live on forever." It was a powerful moment between old friends who had gone through not just time together but also an era in our homeland never to be repeated. Two days later, the man who who would be dubbed the godfather of rocksteady passed away.

·····················▶
Gregory Isaacs

Then there was Jack Ruby, who was another producer with ties to Studio 17. In the seventies, most music producers were headquartered in Kingston. Ruby, however, was the exception. When he relocated to Ocho Rios, he took his sound system with him, making St. Ann the first parish outside of St. Andrew to have a sound system to call their own. The move was significant. Suddenly, tourists would come out from their hotels to listen to the music being blasted in Ocho Rios' local market squares. Despite the distance, Jack maintained his connection with us, returning to Randy's often to pick up his records and do business. He, of course, opened the door for many artists. In 1974, he brought Burning Spear and the Black Disciples to Studio 17 to cut his Marcus Garvey album.

ALTON ELLIS
THE GODFATHER OF REGGAE
1938 – 2008

66 "I was in Jamaica for the first time in 1975, lured by the Reggae. The first place I visited was Randy's, an unforgettable scene that found its way in the film Rockers, two years later. Nothing pleases me more than to see the Chin family still at the forefront of Reggae Culture."

Ted Bafaloukos

Reggae Comes to Town

It was a high-energy time for the industry, with inspiration running through its players like a never-ending electrical current. Ironically, it was during the seventies that the country began to face its most difficult challenges—challenges that were reflected in its music. That was when Tosh recorded "Legalize It" (partially) and "Equal Rights" (entirely) at Studio 17. With sociopolitical and economic hardships now the order of the day, Jamaicans were struggling with extreme pressures that included, among other things, frequent power outages.

But even uncertainty can't keep genius down. In the mid-seventies, a Greek national by the name of Ted Bafaloukos began shooting a movie in Idler's Rest. His "Rockers" would capture the genesis of reggae music when it was still raw and relatively contained to Jamaica's shores. For several exciting weeks, the film crew camped out on our block, which made navigating the sidewalks and street a nightmare. There were wires and cables running all over the street and plugged into every available socket in the walls of the surrounding shops. People flocked to the area, thrilled to see a film crew "from foreign" making a movie about something Jamaican. I still remember watching Big Youth riding up and down the street on his motorbike like it would never end. Other big artists descended on the area: Horsemouth, Dirty Harry, Robbie Shakespeare, and Jacob Miller were all there. Truly, it was a magical time for us, and a sign that the world was now watching. I was equally excited, but the businesswoman in me was also a little frustrated. With the filming distracting our customers, our sales suffered. I'd be lying if I didn't admit that I was a little happy to see the crew finally pack up their equipment and leave. Eventually released in 1978, "Rockers" would become a cult classic.

Meanwhile, many Jamaicans also had leaving on their mind. The political trouble that had been quietly brewing from the late sixties was now bubbling and spilling into just about every aspect of life in Jamaica. As much as we tried to distract ourselves—yes, sometimes with music—we soon had no choice but to admit that our country was in trouble. Many were making split decisions to leave behind their homes, businesses, friends, and family to head for America, Canada, or England. In order to stay in business, we not only had to have heavy hitters in the studio, but also heavy hitters in the streets, for our protection. During these times, I really had to show people the fighter inside of me. However, every good fighter knows when to tap out. For the first time, we considered the possibility of leaving the only home we had ever known and making a new life abroad. Like many Jamaicans, we were torn. We were making beautiful music—in our case, literally—in a country we loved. But the reality was undeniable. We had to think of our safety. We had to think of our children. And we had to think of our preservation. It would take a few years in which to complete the process, but we knew we had to set the wheels in motion. After a short discussion, we made our decision. We were headed for New York.

ROCKERS
Ted Bafaloukos

················▶

Horsemouth on the set of "Rockers" movie.

Part Three

Coming to America

1977-1997

"Overall, I think Miss Pat is an entrepreneur, a real businessperson that picks up on trends and shifts her mind to developing them, and I was always thinking about her critically in the music industry, about that role that she played maybe having a lot to do with her personality. She always inspired me as a woman, because of how she would just get up and go. I think she operates with a lot of grace, and that really contributes to things that would have made other businesses or relationships crumble, but through her spirit, she just kept it going and kept it together. So she's really a very strong woman and she survived a lot. And whatever VP has, she's basically the foundation of it, even what they have today."

Maxine Stowe

Gone
A Foreign

The moment we made the decision to leave Jamaica it felt as if the twenty-plus years we had invested in our livelihood vanished into a vortex. Even though we had a game plan, we knew that starting over in a new country with new rules and a new culture would not be easy, especially for a couple already in their forties.

But in times of need our family had always acted as a lifeline for each other. Fortunately for us, Vincent had three other siblings who had not left New York after first emigrating there: his brother, Victor, and sisters, Daphne and Molly. While we did not relish the thought of living in a cold climate, New York was the obvious choice for one reason: Victor's toehold in the music business. Years before, and at Vincent's suggestion, Victor had opened a retail record store in Brooklyn called Chin Randy's. Naturally, we had been his wholesale supplier of Jamaican music. Already a US citizen, Victor was able to file papers for his brother, making our case a simple matter of waiting until the process was completed. And so on a warm summer day in 1977, Vincent, Clive, and Chris arrived at JFK to take those first steps of our new journey. I stayed behind in Jamaica with Randy and Angela to run the store while waiting for Vincent to file for us as soon as he legally could. It was hard to be separated as a family, and harder to run the business with Vincent and the boys gone, but we managed. Thankfully, Keith was there

Randy Chin Jr. at VP Records Retail in Jamaica, NY

Chris Chin at VP Records' original retail location
at 170-03 Jamaica Avenue, NY (1977)

to cover the studio. But the delay in my departure had some positives. It would give Vincent a chance to find us a home and business, and me the chance to say my long goodbye to 17 North Parade and the world we had created there.

Vincent and the boys were now becoming acquainted with New York and North American living in general. Temporarily camping out in Daphne's basement while they got their bearings, they quickly learned how to fend for themselves without a woman in the house. That included doing their own laundry—a chore many Caribbean men were unfamiliar with. Cooking was another skill that our traditional Jamaican life had spared them. But when the poor souls finally grew tired of TV dinners, they decided to try their hand at the stove. When I came to visit them for the first time I was relieved to find them looking well. That, however, was more than I could say for the pots and pans. I didn't find a single one that hadn't been burnt.

Angela Chin
(daughter) and Karl
Miller at
VP Records Retail in
Jamaica, NY

" "As the matriarch of our family, she has taught me everything that I am today, and I am truly grateful.

The hard work and sacrifices she has made throughout her life are a testimony of the unconditional love that she has for me and our family."

Your loving daughter, Angela

As planned, Vincent began exploring New York's boroughs to find us a place to set down new roots. At first he concentrated his search in Brooklyn where his brother was, but failed to find something both he and our budget liked. It took a little while, but when he hit Queens, he fell in love and ended his search. A thriving area with big department stores like Stern's, J. Kurtz and Sons, and May, as well as grand old theaters like Valencia and the Merrick housed in art deco buildings, the area had a vibe he liked. "This is it, Pat!" he said on another one of our long distance calls. "I've found the perfect place. We're leaving the town of Kings and moving to the borough of Queens!" At that time, Queens had mostly a white population. Race was not an issue for us; we were Jamaicans accustomed to living among different races. Still, I admit to wondering how we would be received in this new land and how that reception would impact our business. But Vincent remained excited about his choice and even prophesied about the change that was to come. "One day," he said, "Mark my words. One day you'll see a lot of Caribbean people coming this way. You just watch." After a little research, he settled on a small rental store near the elevated train that ran above, of all places, Jamaica Avenue.

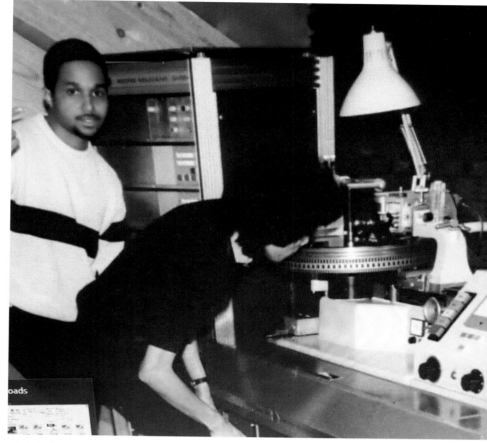

Chris Chin at VP Records' cutting lab

Chris Chin in VP Records' mixing lab

VP Records
retail store
on
Jamaica Avenue,
Jamaica, Queens

"As a woman myself who stood up in a male-dominated business over the years, I have to give it to Miss Pat, because it really started out like that—thank God it's not too bad now—but it was totally male-dominated, all male producers and mostly male dominated, and Miss Pat as a woman, wow! She's a tower of strength and she's such a sweet person, with a beautiful personality, but yet, she does the business. So, someone like that has to be blessed, always radiant; may she continue to keep the fire burning."

Marcia Griffiths

The Birth of VP Records

Still learning the lay of the land, we decided to focus initially on wholesaling Jamaican records until we were sufficiently acclimated. This, however, ended up being a mistake. With only a few outlets in New York supporting Jamaican music in those days, we were essentially putting all our eggs in only a handful of baskets.

Brooklyn's Town Hall Records, our biggest customer at the time, was one such outfit. When their orders came in we'd break into a smile. And for good reason. Sometimes they'd order hundreds of one title, especially if it was a Bob Marley record. So when Town Hall Records suddenly went bankrupt, our sales plummeted and our smiles disappeared. But, as is the case with all things in life, we were paying our dues in a new arena and learning as we went along.

Being practical people, we accepted our position as the new kids on the block with humility and grace and gradually grew a retail base the old-fashioned way. We sent out word—sometimes literally and sometimes by flyer—that we were open for business. We let New Yorkers know that VP Records could access any Jamaican title available. Our name didn't go viral, as they'd say nowadays, but we had small victories and celebrated each one. I still remember Vincent calling to tell me about the customer who had made a special request for some hard-to-find records. He was about to travel abroad and want-

ed the records desperately. He was so thrilled when we filled his order that he gave Vincent a whopping $50 tip on his $15 bill. I think that's when we really understood what music meant to the homesick. To an overseas Jamaican, reggae music had the power to make their mom happy, a girlfriend swoon, or the sun blaze bright on a dreary winter day. That's when we understood that we weren't just in the record business—we were now in the nostalgia business.

Vincent, Miss Pat and son Randy.

L to R: Clive Chin, Joel Chin, and Lister of Island Records at Randy's Records

◄ ·······································

Street scene in front of Chin Randy's in Brooklyn, NY

Flexing Like Bamboo

Meanwhile, I continued running 17 North Parade and supplying our New York store. With Jamaica's music culture still going strong, we were shipping a lot from Jamaica—and I mean a lot. This did not come without some aggravation, however. Because of Jamaica's reputation for growing and exporting marijuana, US Customs officers would comb through every single box. The delay it caused upset us, of course, but we knew that they were only doing their job. I tried to go around the system by stuffing my suitcases with records on my many trips up. But when the Jamaican Government realized that export dollars were not coming back to the country, it clamped down on exports, making our suitcase solution a no-go. Once again we were forced to find another way. And then it came to us. We would press the records ourselves in New York. With no time to waste, we immediately approached the producers with our idea: "Trust us with your labels and stampers and we'll split the profits with you." Much to our delight, they agreed. And so on each trip I'd pack the labels and the stampers (the large metal discs used in pressing), take them to New York, and press the records locally. Once I returned to Jamaica, I'd hand over to the producers their property and share of the profit. This worked out perfectly for the producers, whose export revenue had also been hurt by the ban. Now at least they were able to continue selling and promoting their music to the overseas market. Likewise, it helped many of the country's singers who had no other way to get their music out and money in. Judy Mowatt of the I-Threes reminded me of this sometime ago. "Miss Pat," she said, "you were the first one to ever buy five hundred copies of my 'Black Woman' LP."

Frankie Paul from the Hot Number LP — photo by Randy Chin

Back to Basics

We were now testing the waters in a new market in which reggae music—especially the new titles—received practically no airplay. It was, ironically, a replay of 1950s Jamaica when radio DJs would not play mento and ska. With no connections or influence in this new territory, we did what the small producers used to do back when we were just starting out at 17 North Parade: we hit the pavement. Chris, who was working at the store from day one, had enrolled at the TCI School of Electronics in Manhattan as part of his settling in process. God bless that

boy. He would wake up at five in the morning, take our little van to New Jersey to pick up a shipment of records, and go to the early class before opening the store at eleven with Clive and Vincent. Sometimes he wouldn't get back home until midnight, and yet he did this every day, like clockwork, even on weekends when he had to. Those were the days when he would go into Brooklyn three or four times a week with literally a couple of 45s to sell here and there, trying to attract new customers—American customers. I still remember so clearly. We had a book where we kept an account of the sales:

Judy Mowatt (Portrait by Charis Tsevis)

THE REGGAE HALL OF FAME
CELEBRATING GREAT JAMAICAN MUSIC

Christopher Chin and his dad in New York

$30 yesterday; $45 today. At times we were only making $130 a week, out of which we had to pay the rent, plus expenses. Many nights, when I was still in Jamaica, Chris would call to update me. One day, he sounded particularly disheartened. "Mom," he said, "the people are sending back the records I sold them. I don't know what to do." It hurt me to hear him worry. So I did the only thing I could. I put on both my mom and businesswoman hats: "It's all right, son," I said. "Just take them back and offer the customers different records. Someone else will like the ones that were returned. The music is good—all of it." These weren't just words of comfort. I truly believed that.

No question about it, while New York had its fair share of windy days, very little of it seemed to be at our backs at first. It didn't help that there were only a handful of other stores selling Jamaican releases, like Brad's in the Bronx and, of course, Chin Randy's. Some stores would sell a little calypso, but the only reggae that Americans knew was Bob Marley's. No one knew who Peter Tosh was or Gregory Isaacs or any of those names that were big in Jamaica. That all changed when WLIB, WNWK and a couple of other stations finally started playing Caribbean music. Once that happened, we encouraged them to try other singers. "What about playing some Burning Spear?"

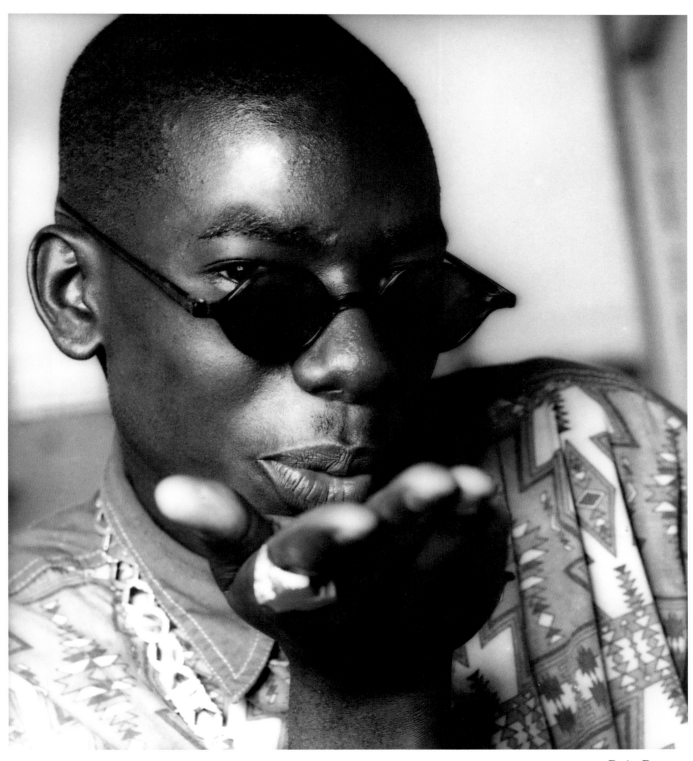

Buju Banton

Peter Tosh

we'd say. Or, "Don't you know Lee Perry?" Because we were the only ones bringing up records from Jamaica, we were the only ones introducing music that few outside of Jamaica had ever heard. This, of course, included hardcore roots and culture. I was sending up titles that were taking the island by storm, including numbers by Augustus Pablo and Israel Vibration. But that kind of music didn't move the needle with Americans. Somehow they couldn't make the connection between those artists and Bob Marley. Our customers would frown, clearly wondering what this "strange" music was that they were hearing for the first time. To their ears it was just too different.

Together Again

My papers came through in 1978. By then I had brought in my brother, Harry, and sister-in-law to take over from us at North Parade. That summer, my children and I packed our things and left the island. I still remember Angela, staring out of the airplane window as

we flew into New York, mesmerized by all the lights and the enormous bridges and skyscrapers. On the ground, everything appeared on an exaggerated scale—like life on a big movie screen. Because our arrival coincided with a strike on the docks, however, we had to wait for our container to be cleared at the New Jersey wharf. We cheered when two months later it finally arrived at our house in Elmont, Long Island, and stood by eagerly as the assigned customs officer sat in his chair watching his assistants pull out box after box from the container. At his directive, they opened the ones he wanted to inspect. Soon he came across one filled with food. And another. And still another. He turned to me. "Ma'am, I get the furniture and clothes, but why do you have so much food?" he asked. "We don't have a famine here." Because in those days you couldn't leave Jamaica with more than US$50, I had packed every single food item with a long shelf life. Finding the items to begin with was a feat in itself. In the year leading up to our departure, basic food items like flour and sugar had become hard to find, and were at times simply unavailable. But I kept at it, slowly stockpiling all that I could. By the time I was finished, that container had enough Grace rice, sugar, flour, tinned

milk, sardines, bully beef, and cooking oil to stock a small bodega. I smiled at him. "Yes, I know," I said. "But we're starting all over again and don't have much money, so we brought everything we could." My family and I laughed for a long time at that memory.

In a way, I was glad that I had brought my familiar Jamaican brands with me. I admit that I struggled at first in a city as busy and overwhelming as New York. I had to get used to the various accents, the culture, and the people. For the longest time I didn't know where my real home was; I still had one foot in Jamaica and one in America. I may have taken a plane to get here, but struggled to cross that emotional bridge while figuring out key things—like who our U.S. customer base was, how to get around the city, and where to send Randy and Angela to school. As much as I put on a smile every day, there were times I felt like an outsider and very much alone. Fortunately for me, I had an aunt in New York—my mom's youngest sister—who would help ease me into my new home. Aunt Edna was a courageous woman who had left Jamaica in her

Beres Hammond

L to R: Toyan, Gregory Isaacs & Dillinger

Toyan outside of Randy's Record Mart

thirties to break the shop cycle. Once in New York, she built a wonderful life for herself filled with a career, charity work, and social network that kept her busy. When I arrived, she reached out and brought me into the folds of North American life. She exposed me to the work she was doing with the NAACP (The National Association for the Advancement of Colored People), took me to charity events, and encouraged me to keep going forward no matter how tough things got. Despite the trials and tribulations of getting used to life in America, however, not once did I regret moving here. I knew that in this country awaited a world of opportunity for my children and their children to come. I knew this because of what I had seen my aunt achieve.

> "The good thing about VP was that they was our outlet. Because now all the majors are buying into our music. But back then, VP was our only outlet. They was that little candle light at the end of the tunnel."

> Orville "Shaggy" Burrell

Dancehall Daze

Within a couple years of my arrival in New York, we were ready to invest in our new business. Taking on the burden of a mortgage, we bought a building that was up for sale at 170-21 Jamaica Avenue. The seller was a wonderful Jewish gentleman by the name of Mr. Kleinholt, who was closing his own record wholesale business and retiring.

Happy to have found the ideal place, we grabbed it and turned it into our retail and wholesale store. We thought we were lucky to get the building, but little did we know that we were about to get even luckier. Mr. Kleinholt's former secretary, Rhoda Bernstein—a lovely Jewish lady—stayed on with us. I don't know what it was, but we took to each other right away. Like Aunt Edna, Rhoda was a godsend to me. A native New Yorker, she wasn't afraid of the winters no matter how bad it got. Even though she was some ten years older than we were, she would simply wrap herself in her winter gear and come to work. In the true spirit of generosity, she taught us everything she thought would help us adjust to our new urban American home. But if we thought we had to help her understand our Jamaican sensibilities, we were wrong. When our Jamaican customers came in with their thick patois, she quickly learned their names, and even—much to our shock—how to rap a little with them. And when the schoolboys were a few cents short on a purchase, she'd handle that well. "OK," she'd say. "I'm going to

Gregory Isaacs

lend you this money because I have to balance my books. But when you come in again, you'll repay me then. Right?" To say that she made our transition into New York life easier is an understatement. She was like a watchful mother to us, working with us every day and sharing camaraderie. Rhoda worked with us for fifteen years until she died. Today I drink my coffee black because of her; that's how she used to take it.

Feeling more sure-footed in a building of our own, we set plans in motion to establish a new label so that we could begin pressing and distributing in New York. We were quickly going back to all the basics that had made us successful in Jamaica, including serving our community as a reliable one-stop shop for all things Jamaican and Caribbean music. No one, it seemed, was using this golden formula. While everyone in the music industry was doing something, no one was doing everything. At the time there were even two or three American-owned labels putting out reggae music. But they focused only on classic reggae or what had become popularly thought of by foreigners as reggae. Because VP Records was covering all the various expressions with-

Beres Hammond and
Marcia Griffiths
....
Below: Cocoa Tea at King
Jammy's Studio

in the reggae genre—including the emerging hardcore reggae—we had the edge.

Week after week we kept chipping away at our new market. To improve our traction, I used the same approach as I had taken in our North Parade store: I studied my customers in order to give them better service. This time, however, the information I got went a little deeper: What demographics were they? Were they white or black? Were they Caribbean? Where was the store located? Based on what I learned, I would decide what kind of product to send them. Before long, we had customers in almost every state. Naturally, we did business with as many stores as we could locally in Brooklyn and the Bronx, and even capitalized on the industry politics. Charley's Records and Bee's are two that still come to mind where this was concerned. While both calypso record purveyors bought from us as we did from them, the two rivals refused to buy direct from each other. As a result—you guessed it—VP Records became the go-between. I had to chuckle when it occurred to me that this was a bit like the game we played with Joe Gibbs all those years before,

Shabba Ranks

but in reverse. I still thank Charley's and Bee's for two things: teaching me about soca music and giving me a new listener's perspective. When I first listened to soca, my reaction was the same as that of our new customers who felt that all reggae sounded the same. I paid my dues and made my mistakes like anyone else, but eventually learned enough about the genre to become a bit of an expert on it. We would eventually go on to work with several soca artists, with our "Soca Gold" becoming an important series for us and for artists like Bunji Garlin, who managed to cross over and achieve mainstream success.

Enter Dancehall

We wanted the same thing for ourselves and for reggae: crossover success in America. But with no manual to follow, all we could do was try every angle. We kept our eyes open for opportunities and an even closer ear on the new music coming out of Jamaica. Back in the late seventies, just as I was leaving the island, a new reggae offshoot by the name of dancehall was taking root beneath the field of mainstream reggae. By the time we finished setting up our VP Records label in 1979, dancehall had broken through the surface and was growing past all other reggae forms in Jamaica. Artists like Barrington Levy, Yellowman, Sugar Minott, Super Cat, Shabba Ranks, and Buju Banton had become household names. Not long after in the mid eighties, King Jammy, Bobby "Digital" Dixon, and Wayne Smith became some of the most influential producers of dancehall music. The big hit of 1985 was Smith's "Under Mi Sleng Teng" with an entirely digitized riddim hook. Many credit this

King Jammy at King Jammy's Studio

The late, great Bobby "Digital" Dixon in the studio

133

song with being the first "digital riddim" in reggae, and the one that opened the gates to the modern dancehall era. But while Jamaica and the Caribbean were jamming to new sounds in the 1980s and '90s, New York was also moving to its own homegrown genre that had stepped onto the stage. Its name was

hip-hop. The almost simultaneous emergence of the two genres would be the start of another massive wave for VP Records that we did not see coming.

While the stars were aligning for us as a business, our children were also making strides. As a mom, I was proud to see them making the most of the opportunities afforded them in our new home, and generally enjoying their lives. By now, Chris had completed his studies in electronics and was fully entrenched in VP Records. In 1980, Randy left for college in Arizona, a step that would lead him to an exciting aeronautics career in California. Bringing up the rear, Angela would graduate from high school and pursue a business degree at St. John's University, after which she'd forge a busy career with New York Life Insurance Company. But even after putting in long days at her job, Angela would always come to VP to help out. Because she was extremely efficient and quick, her help always made a difference.

PHYLLIS
DILLON
1967
THE QUEEN OF
ROCKSTEADY

No Turning Back

While the children were exploring their chosen paths, we made another commitment to ours by copyrighting a slogan we felt was tailor-made for us. The slogan—Miles Ahead in Reggae Music—came about in a conversation with a radio DJ friend in the UK, Michael Campbell (a.k.a. Mikey Dread), who felt that we were in a league of our own. The decision, while symbolic, cemented in our own minds the reputation we had worked so hard to build. And working hard was something we knew well. By the end of that decade, the new store we had bought was bursting at the seams. We knew that staying in the business meant digging in deeper. So in 1990, we made the bold step of purchasing, not one, but two large warehouses. The first was in Queens on 138th Street. As we closed the deal, the seller offered Chris, now a young man in his early thirties, some much-needed words of encouragement. "I know how scared you are to be taking on a mortgage of this size," he said, "but it's a good investment for your business." While his words were directed at Chris, they were of some comfort to us; making two large purchases in the same year had us taking deep breaths. The second warehouse we purchased was located in Florida, where our daughter had been residing since 1989 and running her own small, wholesale record shop. With Angela there, it felt only logical that VP should have a significant presence in the sunshine state, too. Not to be left out in this phase of significant changes, Clive also took the chance to venture out and forge a path he could call his own.

VP Records continued to grow one decision at a time. In addition to the new dancehall sound coming out of Jamaica, there was also a new sound coming out of Panama called Reggae Espanol (Reggaeton). We thought that this unique sounding music could be big, so our A&R/Producer, Karl Miller, produced and we distributed El General's "Pu Tun Tun" and "Teves Buena." Both pivotal tracks would eventually be credited with the launch of the genre now known as Reggaeton.

L to R: Tenor Saw and Wayne Smith at King Jammy's Studio

Mikey Dread

Miss Pat - I Love V.P.

For the most part this is how we grew—on gut instinct. The remarkable thing is that while we were confident in ourselves, at no point did we sit down and project that we were going to accomplish this in five years or that in ten. To be honest, we didn't have that kind of knowledge or foresight. Neither Vincent nor I had gone to business school after all. All we had were instincts, experience, and the music. No question about it, I could also be a tough, no-nonsense boss. But I also knew enough to know when I needed help. In those moments, I sought out advice wherever I could and generally put my faith in the people around me. My philosophy then was the same as it is today: do everything with a good heart so that I can reap tomorrow what I sow today. Because I think that when you get caught up in projecting, you lose the joy of the present moment. That's why I tell people that no matter what you want to do, just start where you are. The opportunities will follow. In an interview I was once asked what my business skills were. To be honest, I hadn't thought of it before, but I know that I was always, and still am, big on efficiency. I like getting things done in a way that's better and faster than I did before. Back in those days there were no computers, so we had to write everything down by hand. That meant a lot of writing if we got, for example, a hundred orders for the day. Luckily, Chris was very good with our customers. Sometimes, he'd take orders that were three pages long by the time he put the phone down. If you ask me, I think our brains were razor sharp then. They had to be. There were no catalogues to help us. Everything was in our heads. Everything. Not only did we have to remember what we were doing on the sales side, but we also had to keep track of the business we were doing with the artists. It was all about working hard, paying attention, and remaining consistently focused on the business. It was this approach that led us to our Love label once VP started having label operations in 1993.

While shopping in a Caribbean grocery store one day, I saw a newspaper headline that caught my eye: "Love from Jamaica." Now an overseas Jamaican, I immediately liked the sound and feel of it and decided to start advertising VP Records with that slogan. Before we knew it, the "Love" label from Jamaica was born. Soon after, the Roots From The Yard label came out as a result of pressure from artists in Jamaica who were eager to have their music sold in the States. Some didn't care if they sold only one record or had no contract with us. "Just put it out and see what you can sell," they'd say. While it didn't work out for everyone, we did our best to help our Jamaican talent however we could. Like I said, we had always been driven to do things with heart and from the heart. I believe that this personal mantra was the real ingredient behind our success. The numbers showed it, too. The ten-year mortgage we had taken out for the warehouse in New York was paid in five short years.

Strength Through Struggles

As a business we were growing stronger and stronger. For this I was grateful. Sadly, I could not make the same claim for my husband. Behind the scenes, Vincent continued to struggle with his substance use disorder. Depressed and

Producer Karl Miller

VP Records office, Miramar, Florida

uninspired by the emerging dancehall movement, he was mentally checking out of the business. As his partner in life, I did what I could to help him, even reading up on alcoholism and learning about the disease of addiction. I think that's when I understood that I was in over my head. I could run a business, but I could not run the demons out of the man I had vowed to love and protect. I went through some of my darkest, loneliest hours during this time. As my mother had done for my siblings and me, I shielded my kids from the truth about their father and from anyone who might tell them. I did this out of love. I wanted them to be worry-free as they went about their young lives. For a short while I was successful. With Randy now in California building a career in the aeronautics industry, Angela in Florida running our warehouse, and Clive working on his ventures, I could hide the dark reality

from them. That left Chris, who was running the business with me. He was the only one who had an idea that something was wrong. Looking back, I see now that I did them a disservice. By not trusting that they could handle the truth, I subjected them to mood swings they couldn't understand. One day I'd be laughing and interested in the world, while the next day I would barely speak or eat. It had been the same way with my own mother when she tried to hide our father's alcoholism. Not being honest with my children is one of my biggest regrets to this day. It remains the only thing I would do differently if given the chance.

Not long after we opened the Florida warehouse, my husband decided to move there to help Angela with it and try a change of scenery. I didn't fight him on it. If this could help him I would support it. Once he left, I made regular trips

THE QUEENS OF REGGAE

to Florida on the pretense of checking on business. My main reason, of course, was to check on my husband who, by now, had sunk into a deep depression. Over the next few years, I would be forced to put him in rehab six or seven times. Aware that his health was no longer in my hands, I prayed every day.

Triumph and Heartache

While Vincent was fighting for his life, VP was about to face its next major turning point. By this time, dancehall was catching the attention of the American market. With a style and sound similar to hip-hop, it appealed to Americans much more than did roots reggae. We could not have guessed that this would be the genre to put VP Records, not just on the map, but on the world stage.

Chris and I could feel the pressure building. I don't know how we held it to-

Dawn Penn

Dancehall stage shot: A young Beenie Man on the mic

Shabba Ranks and
Krystal at Music
Works Studios,
Jamaica

gether, but we did. To this day I still chuckle when I think about our "board meetings" that took place each morning in our van as we made the half-hour-long commute into work from our home in Elmont. That's when mother and son would discuss the order of the day: whom to call, what to sell, whom to pay, and so forth. It wasn't fancy but it was practical. We simply didn't have the luxury of time to stop in the middle of our workday to "meet." By the time we pulled into our parking lot, we knew what we needed to do for the day. We did this daily, putting in longer hours, wondering how we were going to handle it all. I was particularly worried for Chris, who by now was a father of an infant daughter. Then in 1995, after being away for almost fifteen years in an almost entirely different world, Randy decided to leave his career and life in California and return to the family business. While the decision was entirely his to make, I was secretly happy to have him join us. He never said it, but the move was, in my eyes, a huge sacrifice and commitment. Not only did it mean asking his own family to adjust to a new life, it meant relearning an industry that had become practically foreign to him, not to mention brushing up on his now rather rusty Jamaican patois. But Randy was quick on the learning curve. None of us could have predicted it, but he would arrive with just enough time to prepare for VP's big breakthrough moment.

L to R: Dad Joe, Christopher Chin, Pat, and Stephen Chin (Grandson age 8)

L to R: Spragga Benz, Red Rat, Beenie Man, Merciless, and Sean Paul on VP Records' parade truck at West Indian Labor Day Carnival (Brooklyn, NY, 1999)

Part Four

A New Era

1997-2020

" "Without the production, marketing and distribution of "Jah Beat's" finest makers, reggae would never be the cultural force that it is today. To Pat and her posse, I give a ONE LOVE salute for generations past, present and future."

Peter Simon

Big Tings
A Gwan

Just two years later in 1997 we signed Beenie Man and produced the '*Many Moods of Moses*' album. When his single "Who Am I" went gold, it put dancehall in the international spotlight and us right there with it.

At this point it no longer felt as if we were in the driver's seat—the music was. Recognizing that dancehall was here to stay, we signed up more and more hit-making artists like Bounty Killer, Lady Saw, and Capleton. All of a sudden, time became a rocket train.

Before we could blink it was 1999 and we were celebrating VP's twentieth anniversary with a concert and album. As if that wasn't enough, we were also caught up in the global Y2K scare. With Randy and his corporate expertise now on board, VP was poised not just to take off in the digital age but to soar. In America, major outfits like Best Buy and Walmart Records wouldn't carry our releases at first. They just wouldn't take them no matter how many records we had and how many times we tried. And did we ever try. It wasn't until a young new talent by the name of Sean Paul became massively popular with his smash hit "Gimme The Light" in the early 2000s that they started to open up. Because Randy could communicate with them at the corporate level, he took proactive steps to get

Bounty Killer

Moses "Beenie Man" Davis (pictured here) and Rodney "Bounty Killer" Price were vying for the "King of the Dancehall" crown throughout the '90's

us through those international doors. One of the first things he did was to schedule the releases properly. Prior to this, the producers would sell the records before their release date. But they complied when he insisted that they be released on the same day in every country. That's when we got a better handle on what records were selling around the world and which markets were our biggest. This gave us more confidence going forward as a company operating in the new millennium. But when downloading became mainstream, we began to worry. All of a sudden, people weren't buying CDs or records. It took us a while, but eventually we saw the Internet as a tool that would make selling music worldwide so much easier. Whereas in the past it would have taken months for our records to reach our customers' shelves—from manufacturing, to selling, to shipping—that time was now cut down to almost nothing. We

had come a long way since our days of transporting our wares in suitcases. It may sound ridiculous to say, but I think it wasn't until 2003 when we finally understood that this music thing was serious. That was the year Sean Paul sold over six million copies of his Dutty Rock album and won the Grammy for Best Reggae Album. That was the moment we each took a deep gasp and realized—as we Jamaicans would say—"Dis a nuh joke ting wi a deal wid."

SEAN ★ PAUL

Lady Saw

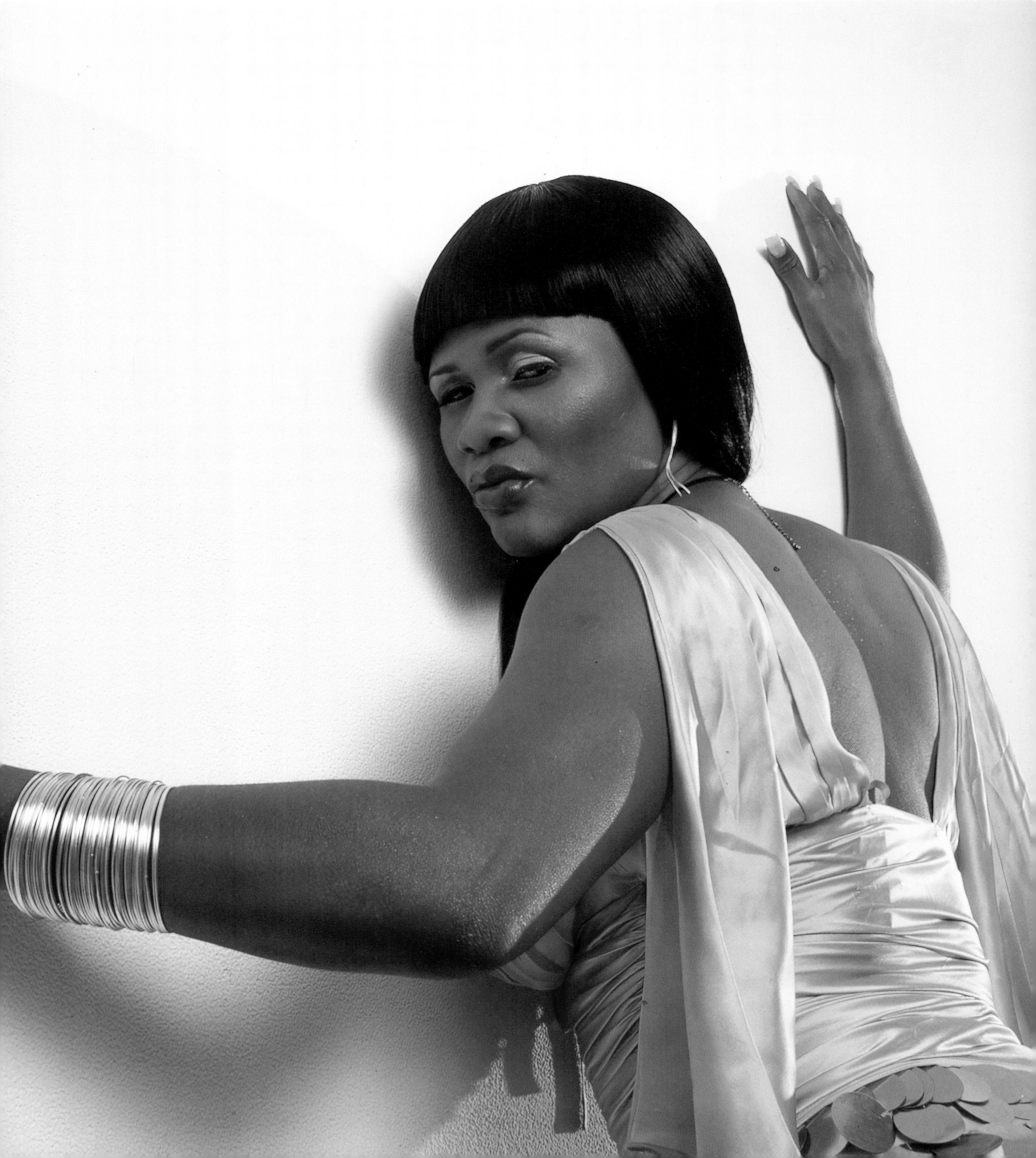

Goodbye, Shining Star

I don't think there were any songs in our archives to describe how I was feeling at this juncture. The business that Vincent and I had built from a pile of used 45s was now at the forefront of reggae music worldwide. Yet all I could think about when I looked up from a busy day—even a very productive one—was the fact that my husband was slowly destroying himself. He had become withered and drawn to the point of being almost unrecognizable. With him now in Florida, however, it was our daughter, Angela, who was living up to her name by bearing the brunt of the last few years of his battle with his illness. She was, without question, my rock when I needed it the most. For her show of unconditional love for our family I felt the deepest gratitude and respect. In the early morning hours of February 2, 2003, the handsome boy who used to visit me on his bicycle lost his battle with diabetes and other related complications. He had already slipped away by the time Angela could get to the hospital. But when she walked into his room, she was met with what could only be described as Vincent's farewell gift to her—and to us. "Mom," she cried on the phone as we prepared to fly down to Florida, "Dad looked young again! He was just the way I remembered him when I was a little girl!" I cried for me and for my children. Despite the circumstances of his passing, I was still incredibly proud of him. My husband had done much with his life. He had thrown his generosity and heart into every person he greeted, every musician he helped, every song he produced. At the end, we handed him over to God knowing that the world was a better place because Vincent "Randy" Chin had passed through it. In his honor, we kept the music going.

Vincent and Miss Pat

" **66** "One of the calmest most wonderful loving persons I have met in this life. She genuinely loves the Jamaican/Caribbean culture and has invested almost all her life into its advancement."

Spragga Benz

More Joy.
More Tears.

Between the ushering of the digital age and Vincent's passing, our world as a family and business changed drastically. Like many other companies, we struggled to adjust to a new paperless way of doing business and, more specifically, to a new way of buying and selling music.

But we pulled through by working as a team. Chris focused on the creative aspect of our company, while Randy worked on taking us to the next level as a corporate entity by expanding our sales in Africa, Europe, and Asia and establishing VP offices in other parts of the world. He also pushed to get our artists better exposure, tour bookings, and promotional events, even attracting some big hip-hop and R&B artists. No one had ever seen a reggae label do that before. In 2003, the same year we lost Vincent, we signed a major distribution deal with Atlantic. Now the eyes of the industry's top players were on both our artists and our label. It was a compliment of the highest order, but one we took in stride. When Atlantic Records asked us to decide which of their two Sean Paul music videos should be released first, we turned to the next VP generation: my grandchildren. No more than twelve and fifteen at the time, Chris's daugh-

Mavado

ters, Stephanie and Christina, watched the videos and made their choice immediately. "Get Busy," they said. "That's the next hit." The next morning, Chris called Atlantic. "Yes," he said, "we've decided."

Milestone Anniversary

The next year we got busy with VP Records' 25th anniversary. Determined to celebrate in fine style, we planned a concert at none other than New York's famous Radio City Music Hall. I was so giddy with excitement that at times I remember it in a combination of blurs and still shots. Much like a family party, we invited several of our top artists who had been with us from the start to help us celebrate all the years of hard work, faith, and perseverance. We had Beres Hammond, Morgan Heritage, Luciano, Shaggy, Wayne Wonder, T.O.K., Beenie Man—the works! Elephant Man was so fired up by the crowd's response that he kept on singing past his time slot. We ended up having to pay Radio City Music Hall for that extra hour just so that Beres, who was slated to close the show, could do his thing. And boy did he ever. The crowd couldn't get enough that night. As tired as I was by the end of the evening, I, too, didn't want it to end. It was the kind of experience you almost can't believe is happening. You're sitting there asking yourself, "Did we really accomplish all this?" Yet there it is right before your eyes. And then it dawned on me: For one night, reggae music had taken over an iconic American landmark. If I didn't know before that anything was possible, I knew it then. Jamaica must have felt that energy, too. Just one year later it elected its first female prime minister, Portia Simpson.

Former Prime Minister, The Most Hon. Portia Simpson ON and Miss Pat

Radio City Music Hall marquee for VP Records 25th Anniversary Concert, May 8, 2004

L to R: Angela Chung (Daughter), Christopher Chin (Son), Miss Pat, and Randy Chin (Son) at Radio City Music Hall for VP Records 25th Anniversary concert, May 8, 2004.

VP 25th Anniversary Concert
at Radio City Music Hall

Buju Banton at VP Retail

L to R: Christopher Chin, Ronnie Johnson (A&R Atlantic Records) Sean Paul, Craig Kallman (Chairman & CEO of the Atlantic Records Group), and Murray Elias (A&R VP Records)

Driven More Than Ever

Only a few years later in 2007, we opened another branch to our music business—our own clothing line. After noticing that New Yorkers were T-shirt crazy, I started printing promotional VP T-shirts as giveaways. But when the artists started expressing an interest in having their own promotional T-shirts, we knew were onto something. If our T-shirts were so popular, why were we giving them away? That's when Riddim Driven was born. Thankfully, my granddaughter Stephanie came to help us run the clothing label. Once she was on board, Riddim Driven became our next-gen's ode to youth culture and its ever-changing pulse and voice. Accustomed to the beat of a different era, I would occasionally question my granddaughter about some of the designs they were putting out, only to remind myself, sometimes midsentence, that I had no business telling a twenty-year-old how to dress. That said, sometimes the grandmother in me would override tolerance and ask my young one to at least tone it down a bit. In the same year, we established the 17 North Parade imprint, the focus of which was to showcase Jamaica's musical past. Both ventures would find strong traction with our expanding international market. But we weren't finished just yet. When we bought out our biggest competitor the following year, we took VP to a level that we—or at least I—never thought possible. The moment we acquired UK's Greensleeves Records and its catalogue of over 12,000 songs, we became the largest independent reggae label and producer in the world. Even though I had been there at every step of our evolution, it took a while for this to sink in. When you have built something from the ground up, the memories of your first steps—of selling used records in your eight-by-ten shop—never quite leave you.

Those same memories, however, were part of an era long behind us. Now almost at the end of the first decade of the new millennium, we were forced to address the new player affecting everyone in the industry: the Internet. While we had taken huge strides in terms of making acquisitions and streamlining our operations, we had also begun to see a decline in sales. Suddenly, brick-and-mortar customers were being drowned out by the iTunes era and competing with "invisible" competitors such as Napster, YouTube, and Spotify. To me, it felt as foreign as getting into a car without an engine. What makes it go? Once again we were forced to adjust in order to survive. Relying on the practice from our Randy's days of buying as well as selling, in 2009 we converted many of those relationships into distribution. By doing this, we became the middleman for the independent labels we worked with to get their music onto these new digital platforms. Now ten years old, VP Associated Labels (VPAL) is a growing part of the business. For someone who had grown up in the days of the gramophone, I had seen many a change in the world. And while I won't claim to understand how it all works, I'm just relieved that we got to our destination.

◄················

Miss Pat at Riddim Driven Clothing's warehouse

Miss Pat on the catwalk of the Target Fashion Show, flanked by male models

Miss Pat at Caribbean Fashion Week in Jamaica

Shabba Ranks autograph signing at VP Records' retail store, Jamaica, NY

L to R: Supermodel Tyson Beckford and choreographer Peter Paul Scott at Reggae Gold autograph signing at VP Records' retail store, Jamaica, NY (1995)

The Next VP Generation

But as proud as I was of our progress, nothing made my heart soar quite like the knowledge that my children and several of my grandchildren were choosing to walk the path that Vincent and I had created. Like their cousins, Chris's children would all eventually settle into positions best suited to their natural talents, with Stephanie as creative director, Stephen as digital sales and project manager, and Christina as co-creative director. Our grandsons Jonathan and Joel also took

their skills where it could help us the most. Like their father, Clive, who had been a fixture at Randy's as a teenage boy, Jonathan and Joel practically grew up in our New York store. Both had an eye for emerging trends, with Joel developing a sharp ear for music. His foundation training, coupled with the grooming he had enjoyed under his Uncle Chris's tutelage, made him a perfect fit for our Artists and Repertoire Department, which he officially joined in 1994. Joel could spot star potential like no one else. It was he, in fact, who had brought us Wayne Wonder, Beenie Man, Morgan Heritage, Sizzla, and Sean Paul. Joel didn't just love the music business; it was his life. Initially based in New York, he would frequently travel to Jamaica with the goal of staying on top of new music trends and talent. But when the industry went digital, he began to feel depressed. He missed the excitement of

Sizzla's album photo shoot.
NYC

Wayne Wonder

seeing the artists passing through the studio and then cutting and mastering the records. For Joel, the music had lost a lot of its original feeling because people were now making tracks on their computers. This meant that Jamaican music was no longer unique. He would come to talk with me, knowing that I understood how he felt about it. "I can't stand to see the culture dying this way, " he'd say. "I can't stand the silence and having nothing to do."

Eventually, Joel decided to make Jamaica his base and get involved with video shoots and scout for new artists. The move proved to be the perfect solution for him. He had met a beautiful girl, started a family with her, and once again found joy in his work. Now with Joel as our eyes and ears in Jamaica, we were on the cutting edge of emerging music and trends. I remember him calling me one day. "Grandma," he said, "Listen to Etana because she's going to be the next big thing." And then he played some tracks that he had just made with her. Joel was so happy. You could hear it in his voice. In mid-August 2011, I had to attend my sister-in-law's funeral in Jamaica, and so naturally went to see my grandson. We spent an entire Sunday together chatting and having a good time, and I could see that spark in his eyes again. Before leaving, I gave him a huge hug. Two days later, he became yet another victim of Jamaica's runaway crime wave. And just like that, our heartbeat was gone. In the weeks following his death, it took all the energy we had in us to even think. I consoled myself with the knowledge that now both he and Gregory were with Vincent.

Miss Pat and Joel Chin (grandson)

A LOVE & A LEGACY

JOEL CHIN

Joel Chin's dedication and passion for Jamaican Music was genuinely heartfelt and an inspiration to not only his friends and family, but to everyone he encountered. He was recognized worldwide as a Reggae and Dancehall Music authority who throughout his prolific career consistently had his finger on the pulse of the latest sounds coming out of the island. His uncanny ability to pinpoint which new songs would become massive hits was truly a natural born talent and invaluable asset to VP Records for over two decades. As the son of Clive and Grandson of Vincent and Pat Chin, Joel was surrounded by music throughout his entire life. Starting in 1993, hundreds of individual artist albums, producer focused collections, rhythm albums, and compilation series bearing his magic touch as coordinator, mastering engineer and compiler were released worldwide to great success. He would at times even cut the lacquer plates in preparation for L.P. manufacturing and edited the actual songs included on any given album.

Joel was a brilliant musical curator who conceptualized albums that sold by the truck load at a time when you still had no choice but to visit a record shop to purchase your music of preference. Way before online streaming services and the advent of the Internet, his role in the Jamaican music industry was similar to that of a radio programmer with a faithful audience who trusted his golden ears. His track selections provided us with a Dancehall soundtrack to many of the most unforgettable moments of our lives. Along the way critically acclaimed albums like Sizzla's "Da Real Thing", Capleton's "More Fire", Tarrus Riley's "Contagious", Etana's "The Strong One", and the introduction of Sean Paul to the world via his debut release "Stage One" are nothing short of

pillars in the history of Jamaican recorded music. The projects he conceived for a wide spectrum of Reggae's greatest artists overflowed with creativity and undoubtedly highlighted the greatness of the music being presented. At the same time he unintentionally gave us a glimpse into his very own special heart & soul.

Fidel "Twice" Luna

Joel Chin (2000)

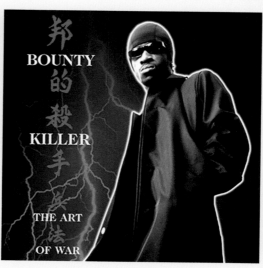

Family reunion in Runaway Bay,
Jamaica in 2008 at the Grand Bahia
Principe Hotel

" A trailblazer in her personal life, business and charitable work, Miss Pat's story is one that transcends the family company that bears her name. This is a remarkable story by a remarkable woman whose creativity, passion and love for her community offers many life lessons for us all."

Dr. Joshua Chamberlain,
General Manager, Alpha Boys' School
Radio

Celebrating the Music

As the family matriarch, I have had to be strong over the years out of necessity. After a lifetime of persevering through hardships, heartache, and hairpin bends in the road, I believe the old "rumor" that women may well be the stronger sex. And while I have rarely surprised others when sharing this opinion, I have shocked many when meeting them for the first time in my capacity as the cofounder of VP Records.

In this male-dominated industry, women are the exception to the rule, especially in management. I still remember the day I appeared with Gyptian at a popular television station in Manhattan where we were scheduled to tape a segment for one of their shows. When the host saw us walk in, he couldn't hide his gut reaction. "You're Gyptian's manager?" he said in disbelief. "Never in a million years would I have imagined a small Chinese woman walking in here with a reggae artist!" And we all laughed and smiled about it. I couldn't deny that we made for an odd-looking pair: Gyptian was young, tall, and dreadlocked, while I was...well...not. But when in the summer of 2015 the American Association of Independent Music (A2IM) honored me with their coveted Lifetime Achievement Award, I received more than huge smiles. This time I was greeted with a standing ovation and thunderous applause.

Gyptian

Music Through Art

I was honored and grateful for the award. Recognition by others for your hard work is sweet and humbling. But while reaping success and accolades satisfies your tummy, seeing the real impact of your contribution fills your soul. A few years before this, I had met a Jamaican artist and activist who had known of our store at North Parade before leaving Jamaica at age twelve. Now living in Pennsylvania and firmly established as an artistic director with a leading department store, Michael Thompson was the person who would show me the full extent of VP's influence on the world. The co-founder of the International Reggae Poster Contest, along with Maria Papaefstathiou, he opened my eyes to a much bigger reggae fan base than I ever knew existed. Not only did he show me how much the sound of Jamaica was loved

and celebrated by different peoples, he spoke of the artistic value of music as a form of expression. And, of course, he taught me about art. Before I met him, I had no idea that our culture was so deeply embedded in it. But as I shared with him and his partner, Maria, the story of my career in music, I realized that we had parallel lives. For weeks we three traveled the world making presentations to fans of Jamaican art and music. Michael showcased his work, talking about how it reflected the local culture, while I talked about VP and the evolution of Jamaica's unique music from the perspective of one who had sat in a front-row seat. I visited numerous museums and art galleries with Michael and Maria, and particularly enjoyed our trip to Cuba where there was a lot of appreciation for Michael's art and for reggae. There, I spoke at a women's conference about

Michael Thompson

ALPHA BOYS' SCHOOL
ALPHA A GREAT JAMAICAN SUCCESS STORY

the influence on reggae by female artists such as Rita Marley, Marcia Griffiths, Judy Mowatt, Phyllis Dillon, Dawn Penn, Grace Jones, Carlene Davis, Tanya Stephens, Lady Saw, Etana, Jah9 and others. But while reggae's Cuba connection did not surprise me, others did. There was the moment we docked in Alaska and saw a three-piece band playing "One Love" on the quayside. In Mexico, while Michael and I were being interviewed on a local radio station, listeners began coming in to ask us to autograph album jackets of records they had bought twenty or thirty years before.

While the traveling was wonderful, it was the experience of seeing our work through someone else's perspective that made an impression on me like no other. This was especially true when Michael used his artistic eye to create VP's mobile exhibition—"A Reggae Music Journey." Designed to look like a tent when erected, the edgy 20-by-40-foot showpiece featured a series of 8-foot panels covered in banners and Michael's posters telling the story of reggae from birth to present day. Thanks to Michael, we were now able to share the history with fans wherever we went, including, most recently, the Art Basel show in Miami 2018. I will always be grateful to him for helping us to see our relationship with reggae. When he died unexpectedly in August of 2016, I knew that I had lost a friend, and Jamaica a special son and ambassador. As if to carry on Michael's mission of celebrating Jamaica's culture and lifting spirits across the globe, Parisian curator Sébastien Carayol launched his "Jamaica Jamaica!" exhibition at Cité de la Musique—Philharmonie in Paris, France almost a year to the week of Michael's passing. While the timing was bittersweet, the exhibition—which also paid tribute to the Alpha Boys School, my favorite charity—reminded me of my last words to Alton Ellis before he died: The legacy will live on.

Michael Thompson

A Reggae Music Journey photo exhibit (2014)

L to R: Dane Thompson, Richard Lue, Angela Chung, Miss Pat, Gilou Bauer, Carolyn Cooper, Maria Papaefstathiou and Rafael Echevarne CEO of Montego Bay Limited Airports at the 20th Art of Reggae Exhibition of the Intl. Reggae Poster Contest, hosted by Sangster International Airport, Montego Bay

L to R: Anicée Gaddis, Maria Papaefstathiou, Michael Thompson at Rototom Festival in Spain

Honoring the Talent Behind the Music

In 2018, VP joined a group of sponsors to help True Tribute Organization honor Jamaica's music pioneers. Called the Jamaican Music Experience (J.A.M.E. 2018), the inaugural awards show caught my attention and that of LeRoy Graham, an old industry friend Chris and I had met in the nineties. When LeRoy and I realized that we shared the same vision of officially recognizing the pioneers, we agreed to help make the event happen. That September night, True Tribute gave away seventeen awards. Among the music royalty guests in attendance

L to R: Patrick Lafayette, Francine Chin (Kool FM) and LeRoy Graham (Founder of Jamaica Music Experience - J.A.M.E.)

L to R: Alphonso Castro, Sultan Ali (Prince Buster's son) Curtis Salmon, Theresa Sterling, Lester Sterling, Pat, LeRoy Graham, Charles "Organaire" Cameron, at J.A.M.E. Awards.

Miss Pat and the late Prime Minister, the Most
Hon. Edward Seaga ON, P.C., LL.D

were Charlie Organaire and the last surviving member of the Skatalites, Lester Sterling. Coxsone Dodd and Prince Buster, who had passed away earlier in 2004 and 2016 respectively, were represented by family members. Of all the guests, we were particularly worried about Lester Sterling. Because he could hardly walk, flying in from his home in Florida was going to be difficult. But when we brought him on stage to the Skatalites' Freedom Sounds track, he started dancing like his legs had never failed him. The crowd rose with a roar to their own feet to cheer him on. While we were delighted, we weren't surprised. That was the power of music.

A few months later, on January 30, 2019, we kicked off our year-long celebration of our milestone anniversa-ry—VP's fortieth year in business (and, unofficially, my sixtieth if you added the Jamaica chapter). Held in Montego Bay, the celebration took the form of an album launch—a live concert-style performance featuring artists on one of our compilation series, titled Strictly the Best LIVE—Montego Bay. After sixty years in the business, I thought I had seen everything. But that night proved me wrong. In the presence of a live audience, we unleashed our innovative album launch at Usain-Bolt's Tracks and Records sports bar and restaurant, simultaneously televising it live on ReTV and streaming it on our YouTube channel. As a global audience watched VP's first-ever concert on Jamaican soil, we showcased our beloved foundation artists such as Beenie Man and Tarrus Riley, along with their younger counterparts. After forty

Order of Distinction
Rank of Officer

To:
Mrs. Patricia Dorothy Chin

Greeting:

Instrument of Appointment

Whereas by virtue of Section 3 of the National Honours and Awards Act, the Order of Distinction is constituted and is to be governed by such constitution as may be set out in Regulations made under Section 7 of the Act:

And Whereas, by virtue of Regulation 15 of the National Honours and Awards (Order of Distinction) Regulations. 1970, the honour of the Order of Distinction may be conferred upon any citizen of Jamaica who renders outstanding and important services to Jamaica:

And Whereas, by virtue of Regulation 15 aforesaid, the honour of the Order of Distinction in the rank of Officer was conferred upon you on the Sixth day of August, Two Thousand and Six:

Now Therefore This Instrument Witnesses that the honour of the Order of Distinction was conferred upon you as aforesaid and that, as a Member of the said Order, you are entitled to hold and enjoy the dignity of such conferment and all privileges thereto appertaining.

Given at King's House and under the Seal of the Order of Distinction this Sixteenth day of October, 2006.

The Most Honourable Professor Kenneth Octavius Hall.
O.N., O.J.
Governor-General of Jamaica and
Chancellor of the Order of Distinction.

Miss Pat at Order Of Distinction award ceremony Kingston. Jamaica (2006)

Front Row L to R: Pat, Maurielyn, Daphne & Michelle

Back Row L to R: Kimberly, Vero, Joel, Howard, Kecia & Randy

Sangster International Airport, Montego Bay--"A Reggae Music Journey"
exhibit. Part of VP Records' 40th Anniversary celebration (2019)

years, we were home again. For me, it was pure joy. But it was about so much more than coming back to where it had all started. The vision of seeing old and new school—past and present—sharing the same stage and singing the same song was powerful. By the end of the Tarrus Riley and Mykal Rose performance, in particular, I had a sizeable lump in my throat. Those amazing artists gave us an impromptu finale I'll never forget. With mic in hand, Beenie Man led the entire complement of performers on stage in a rendition of Bob Marley's iconic "One Love." But when in the middle of the freestyle closer Mykal Rose sang his verse in tribute to us, I had to fight back the tears. "Do you remember the days of Randy's?" he sang to the crowd. I know Vincent was smiling at that moment.

The following day, with the help of the Sangster International Airport's CEO, Dr. Rafael Echevarne, we launched "A Reggae Music Journey," a multimedia display that included the exhibit Michael Thompson had built for us. Beaming with joy, we proudly cut the ribbon, declaring the traveling exhibition officially open. Once again, timing was icing on the cake. Only a few days before, the new S Hotel in Montego Bay had made its debut. This was significant to me on a personal level. The owner, Mr. Christopher Issa, was the grandson of Mr. Joseph Issa, the same gentleman who had given my father his start in business, and whose jukebox company Vincent once worked for. My admiration for the younger Issa aside, I was happy to see his grandfather's legacy continue in such grand style.

Top L to R: Bunny Wailer, Shaggy, "Toots" Hibbert

Middle L to R: Sean Paul, Jimmy Cliff, Marcia Griffiths

Bottom L to R: Snoop Dogg aka Snoop Lion (Hip-Hop Legend), Lee "Scratch" Perry

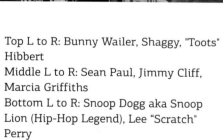

Giving Back

People would expect that as someone who can count the decades of their career on two hands, I am often thinking of the past. And they'd be correct. But even now, I still keep an eye on the future and, yes, beyond. I know there will be a time when I will no longer be here to cheer on our artists with my hands and with my words. This is why I have established the VP Foundation. Through the foundation's work, VP Records Music Group will continue to help preserve Jamaica's music history, make music education available to its youth, and support the country's efforts to promote music literacy throughout its schools. For the time being, however, I'm still very much here. While I may let the youngsters "open shop" these days, I still go into work daily. What has not slowed down is my enthusiasm about the industry, curiosity about emerging trends, and willingness to explore new avenues.

Miss Pat visiting the Cassava Piece Center Charity

Now that I am in my eighties, I still feel as if I am in the summer of my life. Which is why, when summer does return to bathe New York in glorious sunshine, I roll down my car windows to take it all in. I like to do this especially when waiting at a traffic light intersection. But the reason goes beyond enjoying the warmth. Almost without fail, the second I crack open those windows I'll hear the unmistakable

Beenie Man

irreverent, throbbing base of reggae music pumping through someone's speakers. At times, depending on where I'm driving, there'll be several cars playing their music at the same time, turning that intersection into a pop-up deejay clash concert. The first time I experienced this, I couldn't stop laughing in disbelief. "Oh my God!" I said. "Am I back in Jamaica?" At that moment, I thanked God for giving us our foundation years there and our chance of a lifetime here. Now accustomed to witnessing this phenomenon, I no longer react with surprise when it happens. But to this day, when I roll down my window only to realize that it's one of our records being played, my mind hits auto-rewind. And almost always, it takes me back to that young girl whose father wanted her to become a banker and whose mother prepared her for the world as best she could. I think about how different her life would have been had she not mustered the courage to take a leap of faith with the man who had stolen her heart. It had not been easy. There had been bumps and scratches along the way. And, yes, there had been heartache. But while some of the hurt lingered on, we always had each other and the music to help us through. If given the chance, I would do it all over again. My life, even with all its challenges, has been nothing short of a miracle—a blessing from God. And I could not imagine having it any other way. I'm glad I never gave up. I'm happy I stayed in for the long play.

VP RECORDS
60 YEARS OF CARIBBEAN MUSIC HISTORY

RANDY'S ROOTS DUB SKA ROCKSTEADY

PATRICIA CHIN

A REGGAE MUSIC JOURNEY

Front Row L to R: Carl, Stranger Cole, Christopher Chin, Tony, Mike Brooks, Papa Kojak, Pot Skabba, & Bongo Herman, Pat (forefront)

L to R: Carl, Papa Kojak, Mike Brooks, Little John, Pat, Trinity, Christopher Chin, Stranger Cole, Johnny Dolla (JD), Bongo Herman, Tony & Pot Skabba (forefront)

" Miss Pat is a legend. When we were in Jamaica, she run things. So as a producer, I hooked up with her because she's a boss. Miss Pat had the studio – her husband Vincent was a nice man and he was there too – and I just stick with Miss Pat. Then I started to produce singers like Dennis Brown. When I start to make tune, I start at Miss Pat's studio at 17 North Parade, right on the corner there, Idler's Rest. Everybody passed through, all the singers, all the producers. Life was there. We was all a happy family. Miss Pat was there for us. So it started there. We were all carrying the music of Jamaica forward. Miss Pat never changed. She's kind and loving and she cared about the music. If she didn't, she wouldn't still be doing it. Big up Miss Pat. Boom boom boom!"

Niney the Observer

Back To My Roots

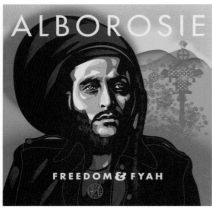

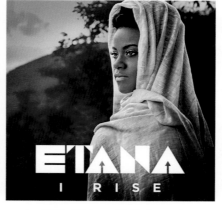

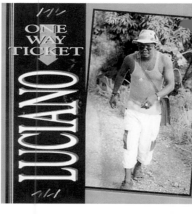

MONTEGO BAY
QUEEN IFRICA

THE JOURNEY THUS FAR
MORGAN HERITAGE

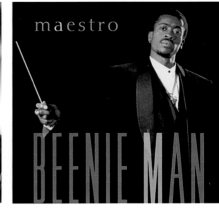

Gyptian
HOLD YOU

maestro
BEENIE MAN

Maxi Priest
EASY TO LOVE

COCOA TEA
Israel's King

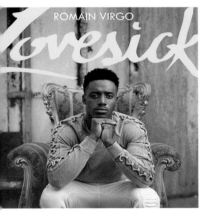

ROMAIN VIRGO
Lovesick

RAGING FYAH
EVERLASTING

1997

Note to Self

Tanya Stephens
REBELUTION

intoxication
shaggy

JAH CURE
Royal Soldier

JOHNNY OSBOURNE
MR. BUDY BYE

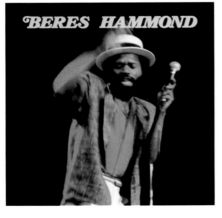

BERES HAMMOND

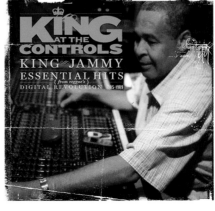

KING AT THE CONTROLS
KING JAMMY
ESSENTIAL HITS
DIGITAL REVOLUTION 1985-1989

We Remember
GREGORY ISAACS

" "It's true that at first I didn't see myself as a natural fit in the family business. But there was always something that pulled me back. I'm glad I came home to the world my parents had worked so hard to build. And I couldn't be more proud of my mom, not just for her business acumen, but also for the mother and grandmother she is."

Randy Chin, son

The Contributors

Alex Lee is a professional writer based in Miami, Florida. Over the past twenty years, she's worked independently to provide clients with ghostwriting and editing services. Specializing in nonfiction, specifically the memoir genre, her recent collaborations include Change of Fortune (V. HoSang) and Don't Abdicate the Throne (Dr. L. Brooks-Greaux).

Anicée Gaddis is a New York-city based writer. During her 20-year career, her work has appeared in The New York Times, Big, Interview, Rolling Stone, Victory, Vogue, V, and Condé Nast Traveler's Concierge. She was the Executive Editor of Trace magazine, Editorial Director of Big magazine, and Senior Writer at Cornerstone / The FADER. She has authored two books with an in-depth focus on Jamaican music culture, I&I and *Small Kings*, with creative partner Alessandro Simonetti.

James "Jazz" Goring is a trailblazing marketing professional with over 25 years of varied expertise in General Market/Urban/Caribbean entertainment, marketing strategy, project management, brand development, content creation, experiential marketing and developing strategic partnerships. From his early days as Marketing Manager & Creative Services Director at VP Record Distributors, James assisted in the development and creation of multi-million dollar entertainment brands. Among his many accomplishments, he created the VP Record's promotions department and mapped out marketing, promotions, and artist development strategies for top music acts.

John Masouri is a well-known UK music journalist specialising in reggae and dancehall. Over the past thirty years he's written extensively for publications in the UK, Germany and France. He's also the author of several books including Steppin' Razor: The Life Of Peter Tosh and Wailing Blues: The Story of Bob Marley's Wailers.

About the Book Designer

Maria Papaefstathiou aka It's Just Me is a **visual designer** and blogger living in Athens, Greece. She focuses her research on poster design, particularly social posters and portraits. Her ongoing project is an extensive series celebrating great personalities of traditional and popular culture in Greece and Jamaica. These include actors, singers, musicians, poets etc.

Maria is the founder and editor of the Graphic Art News blog which was established in 2010. There, she carefully curates high-quality designs, illustrations and art from all over the world that teach and excite other designers. Many consider her blog to be an exceptional educational tool.

On December 2011, Maria partnered with the creative activist Michael Thompson aka Freestylee to launch the International Reggae Poster Contest. It is the only contest of its kind, highlighting the global reach of Jamaican popular culture. The 7th competition was held in 2020. Numerous exhibitions of the top 100 winning posters have been mounted, the first in Jamaica in 2012. There have been exhibitions in Greece, Cyprus, Cuba, Spain, Poland, the UK, Mexico, Turkey, South Africa, China, Belgium, Bolivia, Indonesia, South Korea and the US.

In 2018, Maria curated the exhibition, "1st Medical Cannabis Intl. Invitational Poster Exhibition, for which she invited 50 designers from 27 countries. The exhibition was held in Athens, Greece and the art is still available for other shows.

Maria has received many awards and has been invited to participate in numerous international exhibitions. She has also been a juror for several poster competitions (Escucha mi Voz, C -IDEA design award, Ecuador Poster Bienal). Maria Papaefstathiou's creative practice is motivated by the conviction that design is a powerful tool that can spark enthusiasm, change mindsets and inspire positive action.

Links:
Portfolio: www.itsjustme.net • IRPC: www.reggaepostercontest.com
Blog: www.graphicart-news.com

" I've met many people over the years of traveling to exhibitions for the International Reggae Poster Contest. There are only a few who have become such good friends that I consider them to be my family. Miss Pat is an outstanding example. It was Michael 'Freestylee' Thompson who introduced us. We had recently launched the poster contest and Miss Pat immediately became one of our earliest supporters. She had the vision to see the potential of the contest as a powerful medium for celebrating Jamaican music. I will never be able to put in words how grateful I am to have met Miss Pat. She is such a remarkable person - so caring, compassionate, loving and generous. She deserves the world because with her generosity and kind heart she has changed the lives of so many, including mine. We've traveled together a lot so I've had the chance to get to know her really well. Miss Pat is a woman of amazing strength and energy. She's always the first to wake up in the mornings and the last one to go to sleep. It doesn't surprise me that she managed to keep Randy's Records in business after the loss of her husband and turned VP Records into a global enterprise. I am truly blessed to have Miss Pat in my life."

Exhibitions

(2012)   "Posters for Japan" exhibition curated by Green+You in South Korea

(2012 – 2017) "World A Reggae" and "The Art of Reggae" exhibitions by the International Reggae Poster Contest
in Jamaica, Athens and Thessaloniki Greece, Mexico, Washington, Spain and Cuba.

(2013)   "Innovation for Education" exhibition in Turkey

(2014)   "Nelson Poster Project" in Cape Town and Johannesburg, South Africa and other international cities
"Nelson Mandela Children's Hospital" a Permanent Exhibition in Johannesburg, South Africa
"Jazz wRuinach" in Poland at the 10th International Jazz Festival

(2015)   "ε/Design your Expression" in Greece curated by Toolkit Startup
"W|Design for life" Breast Cancer Awareness in Greece curated by Toolkit Startup
"1st International Poster Festival of Shenzhen Exhibition" in China by Li Xu
"Right to Decide" exhibition at AEIVA Gallery, by Posters Without borders

(2016)   "BikeArt" in Athens, Greece

(2016 – 2019) "Women's Rights Are Human Rights" exhibition, curated by Elizabeth Resnick and exhibited in
Taiwan, Mexico, Poland, Greece, San Marino, Spain, Scotland, USA Pennsylvania; New Jersey; Ohio;
Illinois; Chicago; Boston and Korea until today.

(2017)   "BoobsArt" curated by FactorySeeds in Belgium
"Action / Re-action / Interaction" exhibition at BICEBÉ exhibition in Bolivia, by Posters Without borders
"100 posters for Crete" exhibition in Crete, Greece
"Sing me a song" exhibition in Cyprus, by World Graphic Designers

(2018)   "Transition" exhibition by Autopsia Colectiva, Galería AP, Mexico
"Cultural Heritage" exhibition by World Graphic Designers, Jakarta, Indonesia
"GMO-Free=Green+You" exhibition by Green Plus You, Korea Design Center, Hall (B1) Gallery, South Korea
"1st Medical Cannabis Intl. Invitational Poster Exhibition" curated by Maria Papaefstathiou, Athens Greece

(2019)   "30 years since the revolution of December 1989", Roar 5.0 Exhibition of Social and Political Posters organized
by Atelierul DeGrafica and Ciprian N. Isac in Bucharest, Romania
"Day of the Dead" exhibition by Autopsia Colectiva, Galería AP, Mexico
" World Peace" Intl. exhibition organized by Gabriel Benderski, Spain

(2020)   "The warmth of the city" Zhengjiang City Biennale
"Covid19 Poster Exhibition", Iran

About
the Author

Dorothy Patricia Chin, O.D. was born on September 20, 1937 in Kingston, Jamaica, where she and her late husband, Vincent "Randy" Chin, co-founded the landmark music store Randy's Record Mart, followed by Studio 17. In the late seventies, the couple planted new roots in the United States and established VP Records, today the world's largest independent reggae label and distributor of Caribbean music. As a female pioneer in a male-dominated industry, company matriarch, philanthropist, Grammy winning label co-founder, retailer, merchandiser, and recipient of numerous accolades, Miss Pat has left her indelible mark and impacted the lives of many during the course of her six-decade-long career. Today, she lives and works in New York where VP Records is headquartered. Part memoir and part photo album, Miss Pat is the personal story of this reggae music maven's journey as never told before.

Acknowledgements

I first want to thank my father in heaven whom I choose to call God. Without Him, nothing is possible.

To the entire VP staff, thank you for being there for my family and me. In many ways this is your story, too. For helping me along my journey these past decades, thank you, my industry friends: artists, musicians, producers, engineers, singers, deejays, radio personalities, and vendors, as well as loyal customers and reggae fans across the world. Thank you to Fidel "Twice" Luna, for writing the beautiful tribute to my late grandson Joel and Ralph McDaniels, for your contributions to the music culture and to this book. To my friends outside of the industry—especially fellow entrepreneurs—who always supported me with words and gestures, you remind me that no woman is an island.

Thank you to those special individuals who always cheered me on simply for striving to become the best version of myself. First, my early mentors dearest Aunt Edna and my late Aunt Edith. Because of these two incredible ladies, I learned at an early age what a strong woman really looks like. Loyal friend, Irene, your wisdom and love guided me through all my struggles. To Mara, friend and teacher, thank you for your patience while encouraging me to embrace the world of open lectures, museums, newspaper journals, and the joy of reading. To my cousins, I love you all. Velta, you, especially, never left my side for one minute. I admire your capacity to show unconditional love, not just to your children, but also to those in your life. To my dearest brother, Harry, loving sister, Cynthia, and brother-in-law, Owen, you have been an endless fountain of support and love. For this, I am truly blessed.

Like most projects of a personal nature, this literary photo album has been a labor of love. I want to acknowledge the late Michael Thompson for suggesting I document my memories for the generations to come. My dear friend left us before he could see the end result, but I know he'd be proud. For the amazing photos we have pulled together, sincere gratitude goes to Blue Sun Films, Simon Buckland, Beth Lesser, Ted Bafaloukos, Anderson Ballantyne, Alessandro Simonetti, David Corio, Peter Simon, Ebet Roberts, Marlon "Ajamu" Myrie, Kim Gottlieb-Walker, Roy Sweetland, David Muir, Monika Campbell, William Richards, Gussie Clarke, Allan Tannenbaum, Carter Van Pelt, Maria Papaefstathiou, Michael Thompson, Paul Hawthorne, Johnny Nunez, and Jose Guerra. Telling a story that reaches back some six decades is no easy task. Thank you, longtime friends (you know who you are), for refreshing my memory with stories we shared going back to the days of Randy's Record Mart. Thank you also to friends and family who gave us permission to share their own memories, perspectives, or thoughts within these pages: Mr. Chris Blackwell, The late Rt. Hon. Edward Seaga, P.C., M.P., LL.D, Chris Chin, O.D., The Twinkle Brothers (Norman Grant), Marcia Griffiths, O.D., Lee "Scratch" Perry, Ted Bafaloukos, Maxine Stowe, Bunny "Striker" Lee, O.D., Clive "DJ Kool Herc" Campbell, Mr. Christoper Issa, Orville "Shaggy" Burrell, C.D., Niney The Observer, Peter Simon, Dr. Joshua Chamberlain and Carlton "Spragga Benz" Grant. And because each book needs that all important introduction, thank you, Dr. Carolyn Cooper, C.D., for being the voice that beckons our readers to turn this book's pages.

Sincere gratitude goes to my team of writers, editors, and designers for working tirelessly on the manuscript itself—Anicée Gaddis, John Masouri, James "Jazz" Goring, and Alex Lee, with Alex also sitting at the mixing console as editor until the final version sounded just right. For accommodating our schedule and lending us their eagle eyes, much appreciation goes to copyeditors Dawn Hugh and Camille Lee-Chin, and to proofreaders Chris O'Brien, Linsey Doering and Shivaun Hearne. To Lorenzo Sukhu, thank you for your design skills and for making me feel comfortable at the computer. Thank you, Nikos Glykeas, for giving life to the photographs with your skills on photo-touching. And to my dearest friend, Maria Papaefstathiou, who took care of the layout and final leg of the production, your artistic eye is the book's crowning glory.

Finally, to my grandkids and children—Chris, Randy, and Angela—thank you for going through the manuscript's drafts to help me get some of those dusty details clear. I know you have heard many of these stories before—in some cases several times over— but I hope you have also learned something new about your mom. Janice Julian, thank you for casting fresh eyes over the manuscript when you did and identifying what we needed to complete it. To Aaron Talbert followed by James "Jazz" Goring, thank you both for accepting the role of project manager for this book. Like a true relay team, you made sure we took this project past the finish line. For showing genuine enthusiasm and spending long and late hours working with me, you all have my deepest appreciation.

Thank you all!
You are at the top of my charts.

Pat Chin

To my aunt Pat on her

80th

Birthday

By Gabrielle Hew

A great woman is a force of nature.
In her presence, the clouds recede,
The tides ebb and simmer.
A great woman bears many titles
with ease and finesse:
Wife, mother, creator, builder, co-founder.
Her legacy will live forever.
From the humble shores of the Yellow River
to the island of Jamaica, to Jamaica Queens.
A great woman commands the room
as a conductor leads the ensemble.
With limitless energy, grace and wisdom.
I see a powerful spirt,
tireless tenacity and endless heart in you.

It is our mission at the Vincent and Pat Foundation to support our youth by assisting in providing musical education and instruments to music programs in Afro-Caribbean communities in the United States and the respective Afro-Caribbean countries.

To donate please log on to:
www.VandPfoundation.org

Credits

Photographers

Illustrators